A HISTORY OF
NURSERY RHYMES

CONTENTS

INTRODUCTION 11

PART I.

CHAPTER I. 15
CHAPTER II. 18
CHAPTER III. 23
    THE BABY'S RATTLE 25
CHAPTER IV. 32
    THE CORN SPIRIT. 36
    "CUCKOOS!" 40
    SPRING. 40
    A WORD ON INDIAN LORE. 43

PART II.

CHAPTER I. 47
    GAMES. 47
    MARRIAGE GAMES. 51
    LONDON STREET GAMES. 52
    A WEDDING. 52
    THE KING OF THE BARBARINES. 53
    A LANCASHIRE ROUND GAME. 54
    ROUND GAME OF THE MULBERRY BUSH. 55
    "PRAY, MR. FOX, WHAT TIME IS IT?" 55
    "MOTHER, BUY ME A MILKING CAN." 56

"HERE COMES A POOR SAILOR FROM BOTANY BAY." ... 57
"CAN I GET THERE BY CANDLE-LIGHT?" 59
CHAPTER II. 61
NURSERY GAMES.
A GAME FOR A WET DAY. 61
"ANOTHER NURSERY TABLE GAME, BUT
NEARLY 300 YEARS OLD." 63
A B C GAME. 65
"I APPRENTICE MY SON." 65
AN ARMENIAN CHILD'S GAME 66
RUSSIAN SUPERSTITION. 66
CHAPTER III. 67
JEWISH RHYMES.
CHAPTER IV. 73
AN ANCIENT ENGLISH RHYME
SONGS OF LONDON BOYS IN TUDOR TIMES. 74
"WE'LL HAVE A WEDDING AT OUR HOUSE." 79
CHAPTER V. 80
CAT RHYMES.
CAT TALE OF DICK WHITTINGTON. 82
CHAPTER VI. 84
A CRADLE SONG OF THE FIRST CENTURY.
CHAPTER VII. 88
JACK RHYMES.
ANOTHER JACK OF THE NURSERY CLASSICS 88
CHAPTER VIII. 90
RIDDLE-MAKING.
CHAPTER IX. 95
NURSERY CHARMS.
AN ESSEX CHARM FOR A CHURN, 1650 A.D. 95
A CHARM AGAINST GHOSTS. 96
MONEY RHYMES. 97

NUMERICAL NURSERY RHYME. 99

BAKER'S MAN. 99

CHAPTER X. 100

SCRAPS.

A GAME. 102

MORE FRAGMENTS. 103

A LANCASHIRE FRAGMENT. 108

A PROVERB. 109

A COMPLIMENT. 109

THE REVERSE. 110

CHAPTER XI. 111

SONGS.

"WILL THE LOVE THAT YOU'RE SO RICH IN." 111

TOM, TOM, THE PIPER'S SON. 114

"OH DEAR, WHAT CAN THE MATTER BE?" 115

SIMPLE SIMON. 116

"I SAW A SHIP A-SAILING." 116

DAVID THE WELSHMAN. 117

"MY FATHER HE DIED." 117

CHAPTER XII. 119

SCOTCH RHYMES.

THE SCOTCH VERSION OF BRYAN O'LYNN. 119

A GRUESOME RIDDLE. 120

"WHA'S YOUR DADDIE?" 122

"THE MOON IS A LADY." 123

CHAPTER XIII. 125

A FAVOURITE NURSERY HYMN.

THE LATIN VERSION OF THE VIRGIN'S LULLABY. 126

CHAPTER XIV. 128

"THERE WAS A MAID CAME OUT OF KENT."

A NURSERY TALE. 129

A B C JINGLES. 131

A CATCH RHYME. 131

CHAPTER XV.. 132
    BELL RHYMES.
CHAPTER XVI... 137
    POLITICAL SIGNIFICATIONS OF NURSERY RHYMES.

INTRODUCTION

Without advancing any theory touching the progression of the mother's song to her babe, other than declaring lullabies to be about as old as babies, a statement which recalls to mind an old story, entitled "The Owl's Advice to an Inquisitive Cat."

"O cat," said the sage owl of the legend, "to pass life agreeably most of all you need a philosophy; you and I indeed enjoy many things in common, especially night air and mice, yet you sadly need a philosophy to search after, and think about matters most difficult to discover." After saying this the owl ruffled his feathers and pretended to think.

But the cat observed that it was foolish to search after such things. "Indeed," she purringly said, "I only trouble about easy matters."

"Ah! I will give you an example of my philosophy, and how inquiry ought to be made. You at least know, I presume," scoffingly exclaimed the owl, "that the chicken arises from the egg, and the egg comes from the hen. Now the object of true philosophy is to examine this statement in all its bearings, and consider which was first, the egg or the bird."

The cat was quite struck with the proposition.

"It is quite clear," went on the owl, "to all but the ignorant, one or other appeared first, since neither is immortal."

The cat inquired, "Do you find out this thing by philosophy?"

"Really! how absurd of you to ask," concluded the feathered one. "And I thank the gods for it, were it as you suggest, O cat, philosophy would give no delight to inquirers, for knowing all things would mean the end and destruction of philosophy."

With this owl's apology nursery-lore is presented to my readers without the legion of verified references of that character demanded as corroborative evidence in the schools of criticism to-day.

A few leading thoughts culled from such men as Tylor, Lubbock, Wilson, McLennan, Frazer, and Boyd Dawkins, etc., the experiences of our modern travellers among primitive races, Indian and European folk-lore, the world's credulities past and present, have helped me to fix the idea that amongst the true historians of mankind the children of our streets find a place.

PART I.

CHAPTER I.

"The scene was savage, but the scene was new."

Scientists tell us many marvellous tales, none the less true because marvellous, about the prehistoric past. Like the owl in the preface, they are not discouraged because the starting-point is beyond reach; and we, like the cat, should try to awaken our interest when evidences are presented to us that on first hearing sound like the wonderful tales of the Orient.

Thousands of years ago in our own land dwelt two races of people, the River Drift-men and the Cave-dwellers. The River Drift-man was a hunter of a very low order, possessing only the limited intelligence of the modern Australian native. This man supported life much in the same way we should expect a man to do, surrounded by similar conditions; but, on the other hand, the Cave-dweller showed a singular talent for representing the animals he hunted, and his sketches reveal to us the capacity he had for seeing the beauty and grace of natural objects. Were a visit to be paid to the British Museum, his handicraft, rude when compared to modern art, could be seen in the fragments beyond all cavil recording his primitive culture.

Without, then, any very great stretch of imagination we can picture to ourselves this man as belonging to one of the most primitive types of our race, having little occasion to use a vocabulary—save of a most meagre order; and indeed his language would embody only a supply of words just expressive of his few simple wants. Without daring to compare primitive culture with modern advancement, this prototype's appetites would have been possibly served for the greater part by sign-language, and the use of a few easy protophones. To-day, after the lapse of ages since this Second Stone Age, man went up and possessed the land; we with our new inventions, wants, and newly-acquired tastes have added a legion of scientifically constructed sounds, built up on the foundation he laid with his first utterances, for language is not the outcome of race, but of social contact. As an interpolation the tale of the Egyptian Psammetichus is worth telling at this stage.

Desirous of finding—as the ancients then thought existed—the original language of mankind, Psammetichus isolated two babies from birth in separate apartments, and for two years they were not allowed to hear the sound of a human voice. At the end of that time they were brought together and kept for a few hours without food. Psammetichus then entered the room, and both children uttered the same strange cry, "Becos, Becos." "Ah!" said Psammetichus, "'Becos, Becos,' why! that is Phrygian for bread," and Phrygian was said to have been the ancient universal language of man. Still, however one feels disposed to imagine what took place in the Baby Kingdom of these remote ages, brief allusions only will be made to the veiled past, when either sign-language, or relics, or myths of long descent are presented to us in the form of nursery-lore.

How many thousands of years have gone by since the period known to scientists as the Pleistocene was here—a time when the whole of Britain and North-West Europe wore a glistening mantle of ice, and when man could scarce exist, save on the fringe of the south-east littoral of England—none can say. At all events it may be safely assumed that not till the end of the Pleistocene Era was Britain or Scandinavia the abode of man, when the fauna and flora assumed approximately their present condition, and the state of things called Recent by geologists set in.

Whether the Aryans be accepted as the first people to inhabit our ice-bound shores in the remote past matters little, and from whence they sprang (according to Max Müller "somewhere in Asia," or Dr. Schrader "European Russia," or Herr Penka "from the east to the far west of the

Scandinavian Peninsula") matters still less, "for," says Professor Huxley, "the speakers of primitive Aryan may have been (themselves) a mixture of two or more races, just as are the speakers of English or of French at the present time"; and archæology takes us no further back than into the Neolithic or Second Stone Age, when the poetry of the human voice gave a dramatic value to the hitherto primitive sign-language limitation of the Old Drift-men. At this age, the Neolithic, arithmetical questions arising in the course of life would necessarily assume a vocal value instead of a digital one. No longer would fifteen be counted by holding out ten fingers and five toes, but an idiomatic phrase, descriptive of the former sign-language, *"of two hands and one foot's worth"* would be used, just as to-day an African would express the same problem in a number of cows, and as the comparatively modern Roman used such pictorial phrases as *"to condemn a person of his head."* From this era, centuries before the Celt traversed our shores, "the progress of civilisation" has gone on in one unbroken continuity from the Second Stone Age man to the present time.

CHAPTER II.

"O dea, si prima repetens ab origine pergam et vacet annales nostrorum audire laborum. Ante diem clauso componat Vesper Olympo."—VERGIL, *Æneid*, Book I. 372.

"O goddess, if I were to proceed retracing them from their first origin, and thou hadst leisure to hear the records of our labours before (the end), the Evening Star would lull the day to rest, Olympus being closed."

However, granting the scientific imagination to assume a starting-point when the vast Ice Period was vanishing and language was not the test of race, but of social contact, it must be allowed that the River Drift-man was the first of his species that touched our shores, followed by the Cave-dwellers some thousands of years later; the latter man having his abode fixed to a locality, and his wanderings within prescribed limits.

He may have, this prehistoric man, this Cave-dweller, chattered like a monkey in a patois understood only by his own family; but what is more reasonable to suppose than that the Drift-men of the marshes and coastlines had only a restricted use for vocal sounds, sign-language being expressive enough to meet their few wants? Meagre social conditions, peculiar isolation, savagery, strife for life, call for no complex language, but sign-language has the authority of people living on the globe to-day, not only amongst uncivilised races, but traces are seen in our very midst.

The few examples of custom and signs given below will better illustrate the force of the statement.

"Amongst the Uvinza, when two grandees meet, the junior leans forward, bends his knees, and places the palms of his hands on the ground, one on either side his feet, while the senior claps hands over him six or seven times."

In the morning among the Walunga all the villagers turn out, and a continuous clapping is kept up to the vocalisation of a shrill "Kwi-tata?" or "How do you do?"

Two special signs for "good" are in the sign-vocabulary of the North American Indians, and are worth recording. The person greeting holds the right hand, back up, in front of and close to the heart, with the fingers extended and pointing to the left. Another habit is that of passing the open right hand, palm downwards, from the heart, towards the person greeted. A stranger making his appearance on the frontier line of an Indian camp seldom fails to recognise the true sentiment of the chief's salutation, the extended fingers on the left side meaning—

"You are near my heart—expect no treachery," a most solemn surety; while the hand sent from the heart towards the visitor seems to say—

"I extend hospitality to you."

The "attingere extremis digitis" of the Romans expressed the same temperate conduct.

But greeting by gesture and hand-clapping still live, and are discovered in the first lessons given by a mother to her babe.

"Clap hands, papa comes,"

and

"Pat a cake, pat a cake, my little man,
Yes, I will, mother, as fast as I can"

have a universal significance in Child Land. Unfortunately this survival of hand-clapping, a vestige of a habit belonging to primitive people, does not begin and end in our modern nursery.

"When I was a child I spake as a child, but when I became a man I put away childish things," is a resolve daily forgotten.

In the theatre, when our sentiment is awakened by the craft of the stage player, we show approbation by a round of hand-clapping not one whit less savage than the habit of the Uvinza grandee or the good-morning among the Walunga tribe.

> "O wad some Power the giftie gie us
> To see oursels as others see us!"

This demonstration of feeling may have more *corps d'esprit* than the feeble "hear, hear" of the educated or self-restrained man, but sign-language, especially among the Anglo-Saxon race, is on the wane. Its exodus is slowly going on, lingering anon in the ritual of religions, yet in social life ever being expelled.

"It is rude to point," says the nursemaid to her little charge.

"Is it rude to shake hands, nurse?" once exclaimed a child cynic. The nurse was nonplussed. The middle-class mother answers the child's question—

"Yes, dear—with anyone in a lower position."

"That's a case," said an Irishman on hearing it, "of twopence-halfpenny looking down on twopence," or by another comparison, it is a case of one English grandee clapping his hands over another grandee's head. Still, though educational influences and nine-tenths of the coterie of society wage war against sign-language, ill-mannered men and badly-behaved children must always be with us.

"'Tis rude to laugh" is another precept of the hypercritical mother. Why? Goodness only knows!—for none but a pompous blockhead or a solemn prig will pretend that he never relaxes. But let ancient Plato, brimful as he was of philosophy, answer the question "When not to laugh?"

Indulging one day in idle waggery, Plato, on seeing a staid disciple approach, suddenly exclaimed to his fellows, "Let's be wise now, for I see a fool coming," and under hypocrisy's mask all merriment ceased.

Agesilaus in mere sport romped with his children, and delighted them by riding on a stick round the nursery, possibly singing, after the manner of many a modern rollicking nursery-loving father—

"Ride a cock-horse to Banbury Cross."

With men, however, kingly proclamations, laws, empires pass away and are forgotten, time obliterates their memories, but in Child Land all the inhabitants, from the tiniest crower to the ten-year-old boy, show an eager appreciation in the conservation of the pleasing lore contained in the lullabies, the jingles, the tales, the riddles, the proverbs, and the games of the nursery classics.

And what terrible critics these babies are! What a perverse preference they have for the soft jingle of nonsensical melody; blank verse with its five accents and want of rhythm does not soothe: they must have the—

"Lalla, lalla, lalla,
Aut dormi, aut lacta"

of their prototype of Roman days.

How they revel and delight in the mother's measured song of—

"Dance, little baby, dance up high,
Never mind, baby, mother is nigh;
Crow and caper, caper and crow,
There, little baby, there you go.

21

Up to the ceiling, down to the ground,
Backwards and forwards, round and round;
So dance, little baby, and mother will sing,
With a high cockolorum and tingle, ting ting."

Or—

"With a merry, gay coral, and tingle, ting ting."[A]

FOOTNOTES:

A First printed in a selection of nursery rhymes by Taylor, 1828. A modern well-known baby dance.

CHAPTER III.

"The moon is up; by Heaven, a lovely eve!
Long streams of light o'er dancing waves expand."

The Norwegian explorer, Dr. Nansen, in his address to the Royal Geographical Society on February 9th, 1897, stated:—

"The long Arctic day was beautiful in itself, though one soon got tired of it. But when that day vanished and the long Polar night began, then began the kingdom of beauty, then they had the moon sailing through the peculiar silence of night and day. The light of the moon shining when all was marble had a most singular effect."[B]

Writers on Comparative Religions for the most part assert that moon worship amongst the almost utterly savage tribes in Africa and America, the hunting, nomad races of to-day, is a noteworthy feature. "It is not the sun that first attracted the attention of the savage."[C] "In order of birth the worship of the night sky, inclusive of that of the moon, precedes that of the day sky and the sun. It was observed long ago that wherever sun worship existed moon worship was to be found, being a residuum of an earlier state of religion."[D]

What the early primal melody of thousands of years ago may have been one can hardly suggest, but that the subject-matter of the song was mythical there can be very little doubt, and, like folk-lore tales, built upon and around nature worship; for as the capacity for creating language does not exhaust all its force at once, but still continues to form new modes of speech whenever an alteration of circumstances demands them, so it is with myths. The moon during a long Polar night reigning in a kingdom of crystalline beauty, when all around is silence and grandeur, would suggest to the dweller on the fringe of the ice fields—his deity. The sun, in like manner shedding forth its genial warmth, the agriculturist would learn to welcome, and to ascribe to its power the increase of his crop, and just as the limitation of reason holds the untutored man in bondage, so the myth, the outcome of his ignorance, becomes his god.

Even though social advancement has made rapid strides among comparatively modern peoples and nations, not only traces of mythological, but entire religious observances, reclothed in Christian costumes, are still kept up. Praying to an apple tree to yield an abundant crop was the habit of the Bohemian peasant, until Christian teaching influenced him for the better; yet such a hold had the tradition of his ancestors over him that the custom still survives, and yearly on Good Friday before sunrise he enters his garden, and there on his knees says—

"I pray, O green tree, that God may make thee good."

The old form ran thus—

"I pray thee, O green tree, that thou yield abundantly."

In some districts the lash of the Bohemian peasant's whip is well applied to the bark of the tree, reminding one of the terse verse—

"A woman, a spaniel, and walnut tree,
The more you beat them the better they be."

There is also something akin, in this Bohemian's former sentiment, to the wish our nursery children make while eating apples. Coming to the cores they take out the pippins and throw them over the left shoulder, exclaiming—

"Pippin, pippin, fly away;
Bring me an apple another day."
Surely a tree hidden within its fruit.

In the German fairy tale of Ashputtel, also known as the golden slipper—a similar legend is extant amongst the Welsh people—and from which our modern tale of Cinderella and her glass slipper came, a tree figured as the mysterious power. After suffering many disappointments Ashputtel, so the legend relates, goes to a hazel tree and complains that she has no clothes in which to go to the great feast of the king.

"Shake, shake, hazel tree,
Gold and silver over me,"

she exclaims, and her friends the birds weave garments for her while the tree makes her resplendent with jewels of gold and silver.

"Children's sport, popular sayings, absurd customs, may be practically unimportant, but they are not philosophically insignificant, bearing as they do on primitive culture."[E] Trans-Alpine Europe was a greater mystery to the nations on the littoral of the Mediterranean at the time of Christ's appearance in Syria than any spot in Central Africa is to us to-day.

Across the Northern mountain chains were regions unaffected by Greek or Roman culture, and the only light shed on the memorials of Northern Europe's early youth comes from the contributory and dimly illuminative rays of folk-lore.

THE BABY'S RATTLE

at this juncture is worth according a passing notice, though degenerated into the bauble it now is.

Among the Siberian, Brazilian, and Redskin tribes it was held as a sacred and mysterious weapon. This sceptre of power of the modern nursery—the token primitive man used, and on which the Congo negro takes his oath—has lost its significance.

The Red Indian of North America had his Rattle man, who, as physician, used it as a universal prescription in the cure of all disease, believing, no doubt, that its jargon would allay pain, in like manner as it attracts and soothes a cross child; and this modern type of primitive man, the Red Indian, although fast dying out, has no obscured visions of the records of childhood; they have remained since his *anno mundi* ran back to zero. To him the great sources of religious and moral suasion which gave birth to mediæval and modern Europe, and so largely contributed to the polity of Asia and the upraising of Africa, have been a dead letter, which spell his extinction. He lived up to his racial traditions, and is fast dying with them. His language, his arts, his religious rites are of an unfamiliar past.

Leaving the Red Indian moon worshipper with his death rattle awhile and harking back to Europe, Norway stands out as the richest country in legendary lore, for old-time superstitions have lingered among the simple and credulous people, living pent up on the horrid crags, where torrents leap from cliff to valley. Their tales of goblins and spirits, tales of trolls, gnomes, and a legendary host of other uncanny creatures, point to the former nature and ancestral worship of a people cut off from the advancing civilisation of their time. Luckily for the archæologist, superstitious beliefs and folk-lore tales have preserved the graves of the Stone Age inhabitants of the country from desecration. As in Norway so in the Isle of Man, and in the western districts of Ireland.

In Man until the fifties many of the inhabitants believed in the Spirit of the Mountains; indeed, even in County Donegal and the West Riding of Yorkshire, up to the last twenty years, fairy superstition was rife. Boyd Dawkins gives in his chapter, "Superstition of the Stone Age: Early Man in Britain," an account of an Isle of Man farmer who, having allowed investigation to be made in the interests of science on portions of his lands, becoming so awed at the thought of having sanctioned the disturbing of the dead, that he actually offered up a heifer as a burnt sacrifice to avert the wrath of the Manes. After lunar and solar worships this ancestral worship of the Isle of Man farmer ranks next in point of age, a survival of which is seen in the respect paid by country people to the fairies, the goblins, and the elves. Equally so has the spirit of former beliefs been handed down to us in the song of the nurse, and in the practices of rural people.

A modernised lullaby of a Polish mother bears traces in the last stanza of a quasi-native worship—

> "Shine, stars, God's sentinels on high,
>   Proclaimers of His power and might,
> May all things evil from us fly;
>   O stars, good-night, good-night!"

Other instances of nature worshippers are amusing as well as being instructive. The Ojebway Indians believe in the mortality of the sun, for when an eclipse takes place the whole tribe, in the hope of rekindling the obscured light, keep up a continual discharge of fire-tipped arrows from their bows until they perceive again his majesty of light. Amongst the New Caledonians the wizard, if the season continue to be wet and cloudy, ascends the highest accessible peak on a mountain-range and fires a peculiar sacrifice, invoking his ancestors, and exclaiming—

> "Sun, this I do that you may be burning hot,
> And eat up all the black clouds of the sky,"

reminding one of the puerile cry of the weather-bound nursery child—

27

"Rain, rain, go away,
Come again another day."

Wind-making among primitive people was universally adopted; even at a late period the cultured Greeks and Romans believed in a mythical wind god.

It was the custom of the wind clan of the Omahas to flap their overalls to start a breeze, while a sorcerer of New Britain desirous of appeasing the wind god throws burnt lime into the air, and towards the point of the compass he wishes to make a prosperous journey, chanting meanwhile a song. Finnish wizards made a pretence of selling wind to land-bound sailors. A Norwegian witch once boasted of sinking a vessel by opening a wind-bag she possessed. Homer speaks of Ulysses receiving the winds as a present from Æolus, the King of Winds, in a leather bag.

In the highlands of Ethiopia no storm-driven wind ever sweeps down without being stabbed at by a native to wound the evil spirit riding on the blast. In some parts of Austria a heavy gale is propitiated by the act and speech of a peasant who, as the demon wings his flight in the raging storm, opens the window and casts a handful of meal or chaff to the enraged sprite as a peace offering, at the same time shouting—

"There, that's for you; stop, stop!"

A pretty romance is known in Bulgarian folk-lore. The wife of a peasant who had been mysteriously enticed away by the fairies was appealed to by her husband's mother to return.

"Who is to feed the babe, and rock its cradle?"

sang the grandmother, and the wind wafted back the reply—

"If it cry for food, I will feed it with copious dews;
If it wish to sleep, I will rock its cradle with a gentle breeze."

How devoid of all sentiment our Englished version of the same tale reads.

"Hush-a-bye, baby, on a tree top,
When the wind blows the cradle will rock,
When the bough breaks the cradle will fall,
Down comes the baby and cradle and all."

No wonder this purposeless lullaby is satirised in the orthodox libretto of Punch's Opera or the Dominion of Fancy, for Punch, having sung it, throws the child out of the window.

The poetic instinct of the German mother is rich in expression, her voice soothing and magnetic as she sways her babe to and fro to the melody of—

"Sleep, baby, sleep!
Thy father tends the sheep,
Thy mother shakes the branches small,
Whence happy dreams in showers fall.
   Sleep, baby, sleep!

"Sleep, baby, sleep!
The sky is full of sheep,
The stars the lambs of heaven are,
For whom the shepherd moon doth care.
   Sleep, baby, sleep!"F

The lullaby of the Black Guitar, told by the Grimm brothers in their German fairy tales, gives us the same thought.

"Thou art sleeping, my son, and at ease,
Lulled by the whisperings of the trees."

Another German nurse song of a playful yet commanding tone translates—

"Baby, go to sleep!
Mother has two little sheep,
One is black and one is white;
If you do not sleep to-night,
First the black and then the white
Shall give your little toe a bite."

A North Holland version has degenerated into the flabby Dutch of—

"Sleep, baby, sleep!
Outside there stands a sheep
With four white feet,
That drinks its milk so sweet.
Sleep, baby, sleep!"

The old English cradle rhyme, evidently written to comfort fathers more than babies, is given by way of contrast, and, as is usual with our own countrymen, the versification is thoroughly British, slurred over and slovenly—

"Hush thee, my babby,
Lie still with thy daddy,
Thy mammy has gone to the mill
To grind thee some wheat
To make thee some meat,

Oh, my dear babby, do lie still!"
The Danish lullaby of

"Sweetly sleep, my little child,
   Lie quiet and still.
The bird nests in the wood,
The flower rests in the meadow grass;
Sweetly sleep, my little child."

This last recalls the esteem our Teuton ancestors had for their scalds, or polishers of language, when poetry and music were linked together by the voice and harp of minstrelsy, and when the divine right to fill the office of bard meant the divine faculty to invent a few heroic stanzas to meet a dramatic occasion.

One more well-known British lullaby—

"Bye, baby bunting,
Daddy's gone a-hunting
To get a little *hare skin*
To wrap the baby bunting in."
The more modern version gives *"rabbit skin."*

FOOTNOTES:

B *Times'* report, February 10th, 1897.
C F. SPIEGEL.
D WELCKER, *Griechische Götterlehre*, i. 551.
E TYLOR.
F Wagner introduced the music to which it is sung in his *Siegfried* idyll.

CHAPTER IV.

"One very dark night, when the goblins' light
 Was as long and as white as a feather,
  A fairy spirit bade me stray
 Amongst the gorse and heather.
  The pixies' glee enamoured me,
They were as merry as merry could be.

"They held in each hand a gold rope of sand,
 To every blue-bell that grew in the dell
  They tied a strand,
 Then the fairies and pixies and goblins and elves
  Danced to the music of the bells
By themselves, merry, merry little selves."

To the kingdom of elf-land few English nursery poems have any reference. Our continental neighbours have preserved a few, but the major number are found in versions of the folk-lore tales belonging to the people dwelling in the hilly districts of remote parts of Europe. Norway, Switzerland, Italy, and even Poland present weird romances, and our own country folk in the "merrie north country," and in the lowlands of "bonnie Scotland," add to the collection. The age to which most of them may be traced is uncertain; at all events, they bear evidences of belonging to a period when nature worship was universal, and the veneration of the mysterious in life common to our ancestors. The Second Stone Age men, it is said, cremated their dead who were worthy of reverence, and worshipped their shades, and the nursery tales of pixies and goblins and elves are but the mythical remains of their once prevailing religion—universal the world over. The inception of this ancestral worship probably took place during that period known as the Neolithic Age, when the moon, stars, and sun no longer remained the mysterious in life to be feared and worshipped. In the dreary process of evolution a gradual development took place, and nature worship and ancestral veneration evolved into the more comprehensive systems of Buddha, Confucius, and the later polytheism of Greece, Ancient Tuscany, and Rome, leaving high and dry, stranded, as it were, in Northern Europe, Ireland, and North Britain, an undisturbed residuum of ante-chronological man's superstitions. Evidences of primitive man's religion are seen in the customs and practices of our rural folk to-day.

In vast forest districts, or in hilly regions far away from the refining influences of social contact, the old-time superstitions lingered, changing little in the theme, and inspiring the succeeding generations, as they unfolded in the long roll-call of life, with the same fears of the mystery of death and of a future life. One of the customs of recent practice is fitly described as follows:—

In Yorkshire and in north-west Irish homesteads, and even far away in the East amongst the Armenian peasantry, a custom was, until late years, in vogue, of providing a feast for the departed relatives on certain fixed dates. All Hallows' Eve being one of the occasions a meal was prepared, and the feast spread as though ordinary living visitants were going to sit round the "gay and festive board." The chain hanging down from the centre of the chimney to the fireplace was removed—a boundary line of the domestic home—but at these times especial care was taken to remove it so that the "pixies and goblins and elves" could have a licence to enter the house. In spite of Christian teaching and other widening influences the belief remained fixed in the minds of the rural classes that elves, goblins, sprites, pixies, and the manes were stern realities.

The Erl King of Goethe, a sprite endowed with more than human passions, elegantly portrays the modern idea of an old theme. How he haunted the regions of the Black Forest in Thuringia, snatching up children rambling in the shades of the leafed wood, to kill them in his terrible shambles. The King of the Wood and the Spirit of the Waters were both early among the terrors of old-time European peasantry's superstitions.

Another surviving custom, carried out with much picturesque ceremony, is common to the peoples of the Balkan States. In time of water-famine, more particularly in Servia, the girls go through the neighbouring villages singing a Dodolo song of—

"We go through the village,
The clouds go in the sky;
    We go faster,
Faster go the clouds;
They have overtaken us,
And wetted the corn and wine."

Precisely as the hawthorn bushes were stripped of their blossoms by Maying parties in England in the fifteenth and sixteenth centuries, so in Servia the ballet of the leaf-dressed girl, encircled by a party of holiday-makers, proceeds through the hamlets invoking not the Fair Flora, but the Spirit of the Waters; the central figure, the girl in green, being besprinkled by each cottager.

The Greeks, Bulgarians, and Roumanians observe a similar ceremony, but on the confines of Russia so intense is the belief in the superstition of the water goblin that in times of long drought a traveller journeying along the road has often been seized by the ruthless hands of the villagers and ceremoniously flung into a rivulet—a sacrifice to appease the spirit that lay in the waters. In Ireland the fairy-tale of Fior Usga—Princess Spring-water—has a kindred meaning; she, so the legend relates, sank down in a well with her golden pitcher, and the flood-gates opened and swamped the parched and barren countryside near Kinsale.

In Germany, when a person is drowned, people recollect the fancies of childhood, and exclaim, "The River Spirit claims its yearly sacrifice." Even the hard-reasoning Scotch, years ago, clung to the same superstitious fancy which oftentimes prevented some of the most selfish of their race from saving their drowning fellows. "He will do you an injury if you save him from the water" was one of their fears. In England, too, the north-country people speak of the River Sprite as Jenny Greenteeth, and children dread the green, slimy-covered rocks on a stream's bank or on the brink of a black pool. "Jenny Greenteeth will have thee if thee goest on't river banks" is the warning of a Lancashire mother to her child.

The Irish fisherman's belief in the Souls' Cages and the Merrow, or Man of the Sea, was once held in general esteem by the men who earned a livelihood on the shores of the Atlantic. This Merrow, or Spirit of the Waters, sometimes took upon himself a half-human form, and many a sailor on the rocky coast of Western Ireland has told the tale of how he saw the Merrow basking in the sun, watching a storm-driven ship. His form is described as that of half man, half fish, a thing with green hair, long *green teeth*, legs with scales on them, short arms like fins, a fish's tail, and a huge red nose. He wore no clothes, and had a cocked hat like a sugar-loaf, which was carried under the arm—never to be put on the head unless for the purpose of diving into the sea. At such times he caught all the souls of those drowned at sea and put them in cages made like lobster pots.

The child's tale of the German fisherman and his wife tells the same story—

"O Man of the Sea, come list unto me,
For Alice, my wife, the plague of my life,
Hath sent me to beg a boon of thee."

Unless such past credulities as these be considered it would be most difficult to account for many of the sayings of child-days, and the archaic ideas that have drifted into our folk-lore tales. On all hands it is admitted that it is no unusual thing to find a game or practice outliving the serious performance of which it is an imitation. The condition of a people who originally held such mystic and crude ideas is seen to-day in types of aborigines and uncivilised races.

In Halmahero, a large island to the west of New Guinea, a wizard goes through a ceremony somewhat similar to the Servian village maid's. Cutting down branches, he dips them into the water and sprinkles the parched ground.

In Ceram the outer barks of certain trees are cast on the surface of running streams and rivulets and dedicated to the spirits that lie in the waters, that after this offering they may arise from the depths of the deep and clothe the earth with a cloud of mist.

THE CORN SPIRIT.

Another spirit, dreaded by all European peoples, was the Spirit of the Corn. In Russia especially children of the rural class sing songs of a very distant age, mother handing down to child themes unexposed to foreign influence. It is true the Church has altered the application of many by dressing up afresh pagan observances in Christian costumes. There are several, but one of the songs of the Russian serf to his prattling offspring illustrates this statement. Before reading it, it should be borne in mind that Ovsen is the Teutonic *Sun God* who possessed a boar, and that the antiquity of the song belongs to a time when the Russian peasant's forefathers worshipped the glories of the heavens, deifying the Sun for his fire and lustre.

The translation of this poem of the fire worshippers is taken from Ralston's *Songs of the Russian People*, and runs as follows. Imagine the crooning voice of the old Slav woman singing it to her nurse child.

"In the forest, in the pine forest,
   There stood a pine tree,
      Green and shaggy.
   Oh Ovsen! Oh Ovsen!

"The Boyars came,
   Cut down the pine,
Sawed it into planks,
   Built a bridge,
Fastened it with nails.
   Oh Ovsen! Oh Ovsen!

"Who will go
   Over the bridge?
Ovsen will go there,
   And the New Year.
   Oh Ovsen! Oh Ovsen!"
Another song asks—

"On what will he come?
   On a dusky swine.
What will he chase?
   A brisk little pig."

The present singers of songs about Ovsen receive presents in lieu of the old contributions towards a sacrifice to the gods. The habit is to ask in some such words as these—

"Give us a pig for Vasily's Eve."

Pigs' trotters used to be offered as a sacrifice at the beginning of the New Year, and the custom still prevails in Russia of proffering such dishes at this time. The compliments of the season are commemorated by giving away the feet of the "brisk little pig." The first day of the New Year was Ovsen's day, but now consecrated to the memory of St. Basil the Great. The previous evening was called St. Basil's Eve, or Vasily's Eve. In one of the little Russian songs it is said—

"Ilya comes on Vasily's Day,"

meaning on St. Basil's, or New Year's Day, comes the Sun-god, or thunder-bearer, originally Pevan, who, under Christian influences, becomes Elijah, or Ilya.

"Ilya comes on Vasily's Day;
He holds a whip of iron wire,
    And another of tin.
Hither he comes,
    Thither he waves,
        Corn grows."

This supports the inference that the agriculturist was a nature worshipper. But quite apart from sun worshippers, and their songs about corn-growing, the children of the rural classes in many other parts of Europe have fixed ideas, or beliefs, in the "Spirit of the Cornfield"; their sayings are represented by different figures, "a mad dog in the corn," "a wolf in the corn," are found amongst the many shibboleths of the youngsters playing in the fields prior to harvest-time. That they dread the wavy movement of the grain-laden stalks is certain, and the red poppy, the blue cornflower, the yellow dandelion, and the marguerite daisy, although plucked by tiny hands on the fringe of the fields, it is not often tiny feet trample down the golden stalks. At nightfall, in Germany, an old peasant, observing the gentle undulating motion of the ripe crop while seated before his cottage, will exclaim—

"There goes the rye-wolf. The wolf is passing through the corn."

In some parts the "corn spirit" was said to be a cow.

"The cow's in the corn."

In one of our home counties—Hertfordshire—it is a "mare," and the custom of "crying the mare" has allusion to the corn spirit, and is spoken of in some villages to-day. There are several rhymes that carry a notice of cornfield games.

> "Ring a ring a rosies,
> A pocket full of posies.
> Hush!—The Cry?—Hush!—The Cry?
> All fall down."

* * * * *

> "Little boy blue come blow me thy horn,
> The sheep in the meadow,
> The cow's in the corn.
> Where is the boy that looks after the sheep?
> Under the haystack fast asleep."

The "Little Boy Blue" rhyme, it has been urged, had only reference to the butcher's boy. The rhyme is very much older than the blue-smocked butcher's boy, and in truth it may be said the butcher boy of a century ago wore white overalls.

The former rhyme, "Ring a Ring a Rosies," is known in Italy and Germany. In the northern counties of England the children use the words, "Hushu! Hushu!" in the third line.

The Spirit of the Cornfield is dreaded by children of all European countries. In Saxon Transylvania the children gather maize leaves and completely cover one of their playmates with them. This game is intended to prefigure death.

"CUCKOOS!"

"Cuckoo cherrytree, catch a bird
And give it to me."ᴳ

The people of the Oral and Tula Governments, especially the maidens, christen the cuckoo "gossip darlings!"

In one of the Lithuanian districts the girls sing—

"Sister, dear,
Mottled cuckoo!
Thou who feedest
The horses of thy brother,
Thou who spinnest silken threads,
Sing, O cuckoo,
Shall I soon be married?"

In *Love's Labour's Lost* a passage occurs where the two seasons, Spring and Winter, vie with each other in extolling the cuckoo and the owl.

Spring.

"When daisies pied, and violets blue,
And lady-smocks all silver white,

And cuckoo-buds of yellow hue,
    Do paint the meadows with delight,
The cuckoo then, on every tree,
Mocks married men, for thus sings he—
                Cuckoo!
Cuckoo! cuckoo!
O word of fear,
Unpleasing to the married ear!"

Thus is cuckoo gossip perpetuated in rhyme and song; but an old belief in the mysteriously disappearing bird gave an opportunity to children to await its return in the early summer, and then address to it all kinds of ridiculous questions.

"How many years have I to live?" is a favourite query. The other like that of the Lithuanian maid, "Shall I soon be married?" meets with favour amongst single girls.

A German song, entitled "The Shepherd Maiden," indicates this custom. The words being—

"A shepherd maiden, one fine day,
    Two lambs to pasture led,
To verdant fields where daisies grew,
    And bloomed the clover red;
There spied she in a hedge close by
    A cuckoo, call with merry cry,
Cuckoo, cuckoo, cuckoo, cuckoo, cuckoo!"

After chasing the immortal bird from tree to tree to have her question, "Shall I soon be married?" answered, the song concludes with this taunting refrain—

"Two hundred then she counted o'er,
  The cuckoo still cried as before,
Cuckoo, cuckoo, cuckoo, cuckoo, cuckoo!"

In our earliest published song, words and music composed by John of Forsete, monk of Reading Abbey, date 1225, and entitled "Sumer is icumen in," the cuckoo is also extolled—

"Summer is a-coming in, loudly sing, cuckoo;
Groweth the seed, bloweth the mead, and springeth wood anew.
  Sing, cuckoo! Merry sing, cuckoo,
  Cuckoo, cuckoo, cuckoo!"

The peasantry of Russia, India, and Germany contribute to the collection of cuckoo-lore. Grimm mentions a Cuckoo Hill in Gauchsberg. The cuckoo and not the hill may have had the mystic sense.

Identical with this Cuckoo Hill, in its solemn significance, there occurs a passage in the game of Hot Cockles, played formerly at Yorkshire funerals.

"Where is the poor man to go?"

the friends whine, and the mutes who are in readiness to follow the coffin beat their knees with open hands and reply—

"Over the Cuckoo Hill, I oh!"

The association of ideas about the prophetic notes of the cuckoo's mocking voice—in matters of marriage and death—are pretty general, and there are still further many points of identity in the tales told by the children of India and Southern Russia. Like the Ph[oe]nix idea amongst the people of Egypt, Persia, and India, these traditions allegorise the soul's immortality.

A WORD ON INDIAN LORE.

The old prose editions of the sacred books of India—the law codes of the Aryans—were suitably arranged in verse to enable the contents to be committed to memory by the students. In these rules the ritual of the simplest rites is set forth. New and full moon offerings are given, and regulations minutely describing as to the way salutation shall be made.

Much after the fashion of the grandees or the Red Indian moon worshipper of North America, it is told how a Brâhmana must salute stretching forth his right hand level with his ear, a Kshalriza holding it level with the breast, a Sûdra holding it low—all caste observances and relics of a sign-language.

"A householder shall worship gods, manes, men, goblins, and rishis," remains of ancestral worship. "Adoration must be given to him who wears the moon on his forehead," the oldest known form of worship, possibly, of the Drift-man's period, "and he shall offer libations of water, oblations of clarified butter, and worship the moon." The butter oblation was practised by the Celts! They have a lunar penance, "he shall fast on the day of the new moon."

These observances belonged to a people who, without doubt, migrated from the West to the East. The manes and goblins are pre-Celtic, and have likewise been preserved by those who travelled, as the journey became possible, towards Asia. Some of our nursery tales, children's games, are likewise known to them. The same legends are extant in the East and West, all of which have a common origin, and that a religious one.

FOOTNOTES:

G An old English child rhyme mentioned in BARNES' *Shropshire Folk-lore*.

PART II.

CHAPTER I.

"Oh, Love! young Love! bound in thy rosy band,
    Let sage or cynic prattle as he will,
        These hours, and only these, redeemed
           Life's years of ill!"

GAMES.

The annual calendar of dates when certain of the pastimes and songs of our street children become fashionable is an uncertain one, yet games have their seasons most wonderfully and faithfully marked. Yearly all boys seem to know the actual time for the revivification of a custom, whether it be of whipping tops, flirting marbles, spinning peg-tops, or playing tip-cat or piggy. This survival of custom speaks eloquently of the child influence on civilisation, for the conservation of the human family may be found literally portrayed in the pastimes, games, and songs of the children of our streets.

Curious relics of past cruelties are shadowed forth in many of the present games—some of which are not uninteresting. The barbarous custom of whipping martyrs at the stake is perpetuated by the game of whip-top. In a black-letter book in the British Museum, date 15—(?) occurs this passage—

"I am good at scourging of my toppe,
You would laugh to see me morsel the pegge,
Upon one foot I can hoppe,
And dance trimly round an egge."

47

The apprentices of the London craftsmen followed the popular diversion of cock-throwing on Shrove Tuesday and tossing pancakes in the frying-pan—the latter custom is still kept up at Westminster School. Both bear allusion to the sufferings and torments of men who died for conscience sake.

Dice and pitch-and-toss, also modern games of the present gutter children, in primitive times were the ways and means adopted by the learned to consult the oracles. Much in the same way the Scotch laddie and wee lassie play—

"Dab a prin in my lottery-book;
Dab ane, dab two, dab a' your prins awa',"

by sticking at random pins in their school-books, between the leaves of which little pictures are placed. This is the lottery-box, the pictures the prizes, and the pins the forfeits.

Another favourite Scotch game is—

"A' the birds of the air, and the days of the week."

Girls' pleasures are by no means so diversified as those of boys. It would be considered a trifle too effeminate were the little men to amuse themselves with their sisters' game of Chucks—an enchanting amusement, played with a large-sized marble and four octagonal pieces of chalk. Beds, another girlish game, is also played on the pavement—a piece of broken pot, china or earthenware, being kicked from one of the beds or divisions marked out on the flags to another, the girls hopping on one leg while doing so. It is a pastime better known as Hop Scotch, and is played in every village and town of the British Isles, varying slightly in detail. The rhymes used by street children to decide who is to begin the game are numerous.

The Scotch version of a well-known one is given below—

"Zickety, dickety, dock, the mouse ran up the nock,
The nock struck one, down the mouse ran,
    Zickety, dickety, dock."

"Anery, twaery, tickery, seven,
Aliby, crackeby, ten or eleven;
    Pin pan, muskidan,
Tweedlum, twodlum, twenty-one."

Amongst the notable men in the world's history who have depicted children's games, St. Luke the Evangelist tells in a pleasant passage of how Jesus likened the men of His day to children sitting in the market-place and calling to their playmates—

"We have piped unto you, and ye have not danced;
We have mourned unto you, and ye have not wept."
A vivid picture, illustrating puerile peevishness.

In the thousands of years that street plays have been enacted by the youngsters, no poet's, philosopher's, nor teacher's words have been more to the point. Every child wants to take the most prominent part in a game, but all cannot be chief mourners, else there will be no sympathising weepers.

"Who'll be chief mourner? I, said the dove,
    I'll mourn for my love."

To-day things are better arranged, a counting-out rhyme settles the question of appointment to the coveted post. Like the

"Zickety, dickety, dock, the mouse ran up the clock"

of the north-country children.

"Whoever I touch must be he"

ends and begins the counting-out verse of the Southern youngsters, which runs as follows—

"1, 2, 3, 4, 5, 6, 7,
All good children go to heaven.
My mother says the last one I touch must be he."

Of the numerous variations of this rhyme the one at present in demand by London children is—

"1, 2, 3, 4, 5, 6, 7,
All good children go to heaven.
A penny on the water, twopence on the sea,
Threepence on the railway, and out goes she."

Another and more generally known rhyme of—

"1, 2, 3, 4,
Mary at the cottage door
Eating cherries off a plate,
5, 6, 7, 8,"

is also used for the same purpose.

But are there no peevish children to-day? None sulking in nursery or playground over games just as the little Israelites did 1900 years ago in the market-place at Nain?

Remember the lesson of old—

"We have piped, and ye have not danced;
We have mourned to you, and ye have not wept."

MARRIAGE GAMES.

In India and Japan marriage ceremonies bear a feature of youthful play. Amongst the Moslems in the former country—where the doll is forbidden—the day previous to a real wedding the young friends of the bridegroom are summoned to join in a wedding game. On the eve of the day they all meet and surround the bridegroom-elect, then they make for the house of the bride's parents. On arrival at the gates the bride's relatives shut the doors and mount guard.

"Who are you," exclaims the bridegroom, "to dare obstruct the king's cavalcade? Behold the bridegroom cometh! Go ye not out to meet him?" The answer comes from within the abode. "It is a ruse—so many thieves roam about, more than probable you and your band are of them."

* * * * *

In England in 1557 the boys of London town sang a rhyme at their mock wedding feasts of—

"If ever I marry I'll marry a maid,
To marry a widow I'm sore afraid,
For maids are simple and never will grudge,
But widows full oft as they say know too much."

This song was entered at the Stationers' Hall, 1557 A.D.

LONDON STREET GAMES.

A WEDDING.

After the preliminary rhyme of—

"1, 2, 3, 4, 5, 6, 7,
All good children go to heaven.
A penny on the water, twopence on the sea,
Threepence on the railway, and out goes she,"

has been said, the lot falls on one of the girls to be the bride. A ring is formed
and a merry dance begins, all the children singing this invitation—

"Choose one, choose two, choose the nearest one to you."

The girl bride then selects a groom from the rest of the other children.
He steps into the centre of the ring, joins hands and kisses her, after
which, collecting a posy from each of the others, he decorates her with
flowers and green leaves. A fresh ring is now formed—figuratively the
wedding ring; the whole of the children caper round singing—

"Rosy apple, lemon and pear,
    Bunch of roses she shall wear,
Gold and silver by her side,
    I know who shall be my bride."

"Choose one, choose two, choose the nearest one to you."

"Take her by her lily-white hand,
    Lead her across the water,

Give her kisses one, two, three,
    Mrs.—daughter."

THE KING OF THE BARBARINES.

In this street game an entire regal court is appointed, the children taking the characters of king, queen, princes, and courtiers. When these preliminaries are settled two children join hands and whisper something— supposed to be a great state secret—to each other. This at once causes a rivalry amongst certain of the mock courtiers, and the dissatisfaction spreads, culminating in an open rebellion. The children take sides. Things now look serious; the prime minister tells the king he fears rebellion, and for safety his little majesty, attired in royal robes, and wearing a paper crown, retires to his palace—one of those places "built without walls." The soldiers, the king's bodyguard, are summoned, and orders are given to them to suppress the insurrection and capture the little rebels. As each one is taken prisoner the soldiers ask—

"Will you surrender? Oh, will you surrender
    To the King of the Barbarines?"

During the struggle reinforcements come up from the rebel camp and try to beat off the king's soldiers, exclaiming—

"We won't surrender, we won't surrender
    To the King of the Barbarines."

"We'll make you surrender, we'll make you surrender
    To the King of the Barbarines."

"You can't make us surrender, you can't make us surrender
    To the King of the Barbarines."

"We'll go to the King, we'll go to the King,
    To the King of the Barbarines."

"You can go to the King, you can go to the King,
    To the King of the Barbarines."

The rebels now build an imaginary castle by joining hands. The king's soldiers surround the place, and after a skirmish break it down.

"We'll break down your castle, we'll break down your castle
    For the King of the Barbarines."

A LANCASHIRE ROUND GAME.

Two rows of lassies and lads face each other; the boys, hand in hand, move backwards and forwards towards the girls, saying—

"I've got gold, and I've got silver,
I've got copper, and I've got brass,
I've got all the world can give me,
All I want is a nice young lass."

"Fly to the east, fly to the west,
Fly to the one you love the best."

In the scramble which takes place the young lass of each one's choice is seized. A ring is formed, and a rollicking dance takes places to the characteristic chorus of—

"Fol th' riddle, I do, I do, I do;
Fol th' riddle, I do, I do, dey."

ROUND GAME OF THE MULBERRY BUSH.

"Here we go round the mulberry bush,
The mulberry bush, the mulberry bush;
Here we go round the mulberry bush
On a cold and frosty morning.

"This is the way we wash our hands,
We wash our hands, we wash our hands;
This is the way we wash our hands
On a cold and frosty morning.

"This is the way we do our hair," etc.

"This is the way we mend our shoes," etc.

"This is the way we scrub our clothes," etc.

"This is the way we dust our room," etc.

"PRAY, MR. FOX, WHAT TIME IS IT?"

A child stands on a hillock, or slightly elevated ground. A party of children, hand in hand, approach him whom they denominate Mr. Fox with the question—

"Pray, Mr. Fox, what time is it?"

"One o'clock," answers Mr. Fox.

They are safe and fall back to their den.

Making another venture they repeat the question.

"Twelve o'clock," shouts Mr. Fox, at the same time bounding towards them and scattering them in all directions. Those he can catch before they get back to their den are his prisoners, and the game is played until one remains, who of course becomes the fox.

"Twelve o'clock," it is to be observed, is the sly, foxy answer to the question, "Pray, Mr. Fox, what time is it?"

"One," "two," "three," "four," etc., are but evasive replies.

"MOTHER, BUY ME A MILKING CAN."

A boisterous game, played by girls, especially favoured in Paddington and Marylebone.

"Mother, buy me a milking can, A, I, O.
    Where's the money to come from, A, I, O?
Sell my father's feather bed.
    Where must your father sleep?
Sleep in the boys' bed.
    Where will the boys sleep?
Sleep in the cradle.
    Where will the baby sleep?
Sleep in the thimble.
    What shall I sew with?
Sew with the poker.
    Suppose I burn myself?
Serve you right."

At the time of saying "serve you right" all the children scamper away from the girl who acts the part of mother. It is little more than a mild reproof on the over-indulgent mother who would sell or give anything to satisfy the fancies of her children, and the "serve you right" is a girl's idea of what a foolish mother deserves—less impudent than corrective.

* * * * *

The town and country boys' game of

"Bell horses, bell horses, what time of day,
One o'clock, two o'clock, three and away,"

comes into fashion with all the reckless frivolity of early years, when the old English festivities of Maying take place, reminding one of the old custom of bringing the May-pole from the neighbouring woods, when each of the eighty oxen yoked to the May-pole waggon had a nosegay of wild-flowers tied to the horns.

"HERE COMES A POOR SAILOR FROM BOTANY BAY."

"Here comes a poor sailor from Botany Bay;
Pray, what are you going to give him to-day?"

is played as a preliminary game to decide who shall join sides in the coming tug-of-war.

The chief delight of the youngsters playing "Here comes a poor sailor," is in putting and answering questions. All are warned before replying.

"You must say neither 'Yes,' 'No,' 'Nay,'
'Black,' 'White,' or 'Grey.'—
Now what are you going to give him to-day?"

"A pair of boots."

"What colour are they?"

"Brown."

"Have you anything else to give him?"

"I think so; I'll go and see."

"What colour is it?"

"Red."

"What is this made of?" pointing to a coat or other article.

"Cloth."

"And the colour?"

"Brown."

"Have you anything else to give him?"

"I don't think so."

"Would you like a sweet?"

"Yes."

The examination is finished, for one of the fatal replies has been given. The child who exclaimed "Yes" goes to a den. After taking all the children through the same form of questioning the youngsters are found divided into two classes, those who avoided answering in the prohibited terms, "Yes," "No," "Nay," "Black," "White," "Grey," and the little culprits in the den or prison who have failed in the examination. The tug-of-war now begins, either class being pitted against the other. No rope is used; arms are entwined round waists, skirts pulled, or coat-tails taken hold of.

"CAN I GET THERE BY CANDLE-LIGHT?"

This is one of the most universally played chain games in the British Isles. It belongs as much to the child with a rich Dublin brogue as to the Cockney boy, one thing being altered in the verse—the place, "How many miles to Wexford or Dublin" being substituted for Wimbledon. Coventry and Burslem take the child fancy in the North of England.

It probably dates from Tudor times. The expression, "Can I get there by candle-light?" and "He went out of town as far as a farthing candle would light him," were amongst the common sayings of the people of Elizabeth's time.

"How many miles to Wimbledon?
    Three score and ten.
Can I get there by candle-light?
    Yes! and back again.
Then open the gates and let me go.
    Not without a beck and a bow.
Here's a beck and there's a bow;
Now open the gates and we'll all pass thro'."

The chain of children first formed to play this game is re-formed into two smaller ones. Hands are then uplifted by one of the sides to form an archway; the other children, marching in single file, approach the sentinel near the gateway of arched hands and ask—

"How many miles to Wimbledon?"

The answer is given—

"Three score and ten," etc.

When the gates are opened those who are alert enough pass through, but others are caught and made prisoners.

CHAPTER II.

NURSERY GAMES.

A GAME FOR A WET DAY.

"Cows and horses walk on four legs,
Little children walk on two legs;
Fishes swim in water clear,
Birds fly up into the air.
One, two, three, four, five,
Catching fishes all alive.
Why did you let them go?
Because they bit my finger so.
Which finger did they bite?
This little finger on the right."

The enthusiasm with which children of all ages play this somewhat noisy game can hardly be imagined. Try it, you fun-loving parents, and be rewarded by the tears of joy their mirth and laughter will cause.

It is played after this fashion. However, it will not be amiss to remove the tea-things before anything is attempted. All seated, the parent or nurse then places the first and second fingers of each hand on the coverlet, the youngsters imitating her. Everybody's fingers are now moved up and down in a perpendicular way, like the needle of a sewing machine. All singing—

"Cows and horses walk on four legs."

The next line requires a change, only one finger on each hand being used, and—

"Little children walk on two legs" *(sung)*.

* * * * *

"Fishes swim in water clear"

demands the waving of arms horizontally, to imitate the action of swimming in water.

"Birds fly up into the air."

When this line is sung the hands are held up, and moved from the wrists like the wings of birds flapping in the air.

"One, two, three, four, five"

is said to the clapping of hands.

"Catching fishes all alive"

is sung to the action of grabbing at supposed fishes with the fingers.

"Why did you let them go?"

Everybody shakes their head and replies—

"Because they bit my finger so!"
"Which finger did they bite?"

Holding up the little finger, you answer—

"This little finger on the right!"

"ANOTHER NURSERY TABLE GAME, BUT NEARLY 300 YEARS OLD."

Some of the thousands of the nursery tales in vogue come to us without a trace as to their origin. In James I.'s time the ending of ballads ran with a tuneful

"Fa, la, la, la, lal, de."

A collection of ballads in book-form by John Hilton, and called "Garlands," are also described as the "Ayres and Fa las" in the title-page.

Halliwell gives "The tale of two birds sitting on a stone" the same date. It is scarcely a tale, but a game still played by all classes of children—

"There were two birds sitting on a stone,
    Fa, la, la, la, lal, de.
One flew away, and then there was one,
    Fa, la, la, la, lal, de.
The other flew after, and then there was none,
    Fa, la, la, la, lal, de.
And so the poor stone was left all alone,
    Fa, la, la, la, lal, de!"

The way boys play it may be briefly told as follows:—Pieces of paper are wetted and fixed on the fingers, the first finger of each hand. Being thus ornamented, they are placed on the table or knee, and the rhyme repeated—

"There were two birds sitting on a stone."

Then by a sudden upward movement, throwing the paper on one finger, as it were, over the shoulder, the next finger—the second—is substituted for it, and the hand is again brought down and placed beside the remaining paper bird—

"Fa, la, la, la, lal, de."
"One flew away, and then there was one."

The same sleight-of-hand is gone through with the other finger—

"The other flew away, and then there was none,
    And so the poor stone was left all alone."

Another but more modern game, embodying the same idea, is told in—

"There were two blackbirds sitting on a hill,
One named Jack and the other named Jyll.
Fly away, Jack, fly away, Jyll.
Come again, Jack, come again, Jyll"—

to the wonderment of the child watching the quick change of fingers.
    It is the earliest sleight-of-hand trick taught to the nursery child.

A B C GAME.

A spirited game may be played after this fashion. All seated round the table or fireplace. One child sings a solo—a verse of some nursery rhyme. For instance—

"Hi diddle diddle,
        The cat and the fiddle,
    The cow jumped over the moon;
The little dog laughed to see such fine sport,
    And the dish ran away with the spoon."

A chorus of voices takes up the tune and the solo is repeated, after which the alphabet is sung through, and the last letter, Z, sustained and repeated again and again, to bother the next child whose turn it now is to sing the next solo. The new solo must be a nursery rhyme not hitherto sung by any of the company. If unable to supply a fresh rhyme the child stands out of the game and pays forfeit.

"I APPRENTICE MY SON."

In another parlour game of a rather interesting kind the youngest in the room begins by saying—

"I apprentice my son to a butcher; the first thing he sold was a pound of M."

Each has a turn to guess what M may stand for—some kind of meat the butcher usually sells. Should the first person in the circle guess the correct meaning, it becomes his or her turn to ask the next question. Baker or grocer, chemist or draper, in fact any trade may be selected by the person whose turn it is to put the question.

AN ARMENIAN CHILD'S GAME

of a thousand years ago is still played by the Christian children of Asia. Like our Western street games of tops and tip-cats it perpetuates the cruelties of the persecutions which their ancestors suffered, a most terrible instance of the child's game outliving the serious performance of that which it represented. The frontier of the Armenian kingdom had been destroyed by one of the Christian Byzantine emperors, thus enabling the Seljouck Turks to pass through the Armenian kingdom, and deal out to the unoffending Asiatic Christians the terrors of pillage by firing their peaceful homesteads. England, France, and Germany have a modification of the game. In France the youngsters hand round a burning faggot, exclaiming—

"Petit bonhomme vit encore."

German children play a similar game with a stick instead of a firebrand, and Halliwell gives the rhyme describing the English game as—

"Jack's alive and in very good health,
If he die in your hand you must look to yourself."

RUSSIAN SUPERSTITION.

An old custom of the Russian maiden—identical with the English girl's habit on St. Valentine's Day—is still in vogue. Going into the street she asks the first man she meets his Christian name, believing that her future husband will be sure to bear the same.

CHAPTER III.

JEWISH RHYMES.

Sports, games, and amusements were unknown until a late day in Jewish history. Within the walls of Jerusalem, or indeed throughout the whole length of Palestine, no theatre, circus, hippodrome, nor even gallery was to be found, until Jason, the Greek-Jew of the Maccabees dynasty, became ruler, and built a place of exercise under the very tower of the Temple itself. (2 Macc. iv. 10-14.) Herod subsequently completed what Jason had begun, and erected a hippodrome within the Holy City to the delight of the younger Hebrews, later building another at Cæsarea.

Even the festivals were not of Mosaic appointment, and it is not difficult to understand how certain gloomy censors and theologians condemn merriment. To serve the Lord with gladness was quite an after-thought of the Israelitish leaders and teachers. But when the great fairs or wakes of the whole nation were held, pastimes and diversions crept in similar to the merry meetings of our own times, and religion, commerce, and amusement became the cardinal features of the great Jewish fairs.

The Guy Fawkes Festival of Judaism, the Purim Feast, appointed by Esther and Mordecai, commemorating deliverance from massacre which Hamar had determined by lot against them, gave occasion for relaxation. Even the most austere and gloomy rejoiced, while the younger people abandoned themselves to dissolute mirth, opposite sexes dressing up in the clothes of each other; a habit at present in favour amongst the coster fraternity of East London on Bank Holidays. The Jews were a peculiar people. No old-time imagery of the older nations enchanted them; they were carefully taught to live for themselves and by themselves, but to make their profit out of others whenever possible to do so. The spoiling of the Egyptians took place more than once in their history. Whatever nation they colonised amongst had to enforce strict laws and rigid punishments in defence of their own less shrewd people.

Even their nursery rhymes are distinctive, full of religious and national sentiment, and may be counted on the fingers of one hand. They necessarily know the ones in common use belonging to the country of their adoption, but so important are the two Hebrew rhymes considered to be that every pious Jew teaches his child their significance. A translation of the principal one, found in the Sepher Haggadah, a Hebrew hymn in the Chaldee language, runs thus:—

Recitative.

"A kid, a kid, my father bought
For two pieces of money—A kid! a kid!

* * * * *

Then came the cat and ate the kid
That my father bought for two pieces of money.
Then came the dog and bit the cat that ate the kid that my father bought for two pieces of money.
Then came the staff and beat the dog that bit the cat, etc.
Then came the fire that burned the staff, that beat the dog, that bit the cat, that ate the kid, etc.
Then came the water and quenched the fire, that burned the staff, that beat the dog, that bit the cat, that ate the kid, etc.
Then came the ox and drank the water, etc.

Then came the butcher and slew the ox, that drank the water, etc.

Then came the Angel of Death and killed the butcher, etc.

Then came the Holy One, Blessed be He! and slew the Angel of Death, that killed the butcher, that slew the ox, that drank the water, that quenched the fire, that burned the staff, that beat the dog, that bit the cat, that ate the kid, that my father bought for two pieces of money—A kid! a kid!"

Now for the interpretation—for it is a historical and a prophetic nursery rhyme. The kid which Jehovah the father purchased denotes the select Hebrew race; the two pieces of money represent Moses and Aaron; the cat signifies the Assyrians, by whom the ten tribes were taken into captivity; the dog is representative of the Babylonians; the staff typifies the Persians; the fire is Alexander the Great at the head of the Grecian Empire; the water the Roman domination over the Jews; the ox the Saracens who subdued the Holy Land and brought it under the Caliph; the butcher is a symbol of the Crusaders' slaughter; the Angel of Death the Turkish power; the last stanza is to show that God will take vengeance on the Turks when Israel will again become a fixed nation and occupy Palestine. The Edomites (the Europeans) will combine and drive out the Turks.

Everyone, big and little, will recognise the source of the nursery fable of "The house that Jack built."

"This is the house that Jack built.

This is the malt that lay in the house that Jack built.

This is the rat that ate the malt that lay in the house, etc.

This is the cat that killed the rat that ate the malt, etc.

This is the dog that worried the cat that killed the rat, etc.

This is the cow with a crumpled horn that tossed the little dog over the barn, that worried the cat that killed the rat, etc.

This is the maiden all forlorn that milked the cow with a crumpled horn, that tossed the little dog over the barn, etc.

This is the man all tatters and torn, that kissed the maiden all forlorn, that milked the cow with a crumpled horn, etc.

This is the priest all shaven and shorn, that married the man all tatters and torn to the maiden all forlorn, etc.

This is the cock that crowed in the morn, that wakened the priest all shaven and shorn, that married the man, etc.

This is the farmer sowing his corn, that fed the cock that crowed in the morn, that wakened the priest all shaven and shorn, that married the man all tatters and torn unto the maiden all forlorn, that milked the cow with a crumpled horn, that tossed the little dog over the barn, that worried the cat, that killed the rat, that ate the malt, that lay in the house that Jack built."

A Scotch and North of England nursery tale, two centuries old, is cast in the same mould, or rather built on the hymn of the Hebrews found in the Sepher Haggadah. It is given below.

"There was an old woman swept her house and found a silver penny,
And she went to market and bought a kid;
But when she came to drive it home kid would not go.
She went a little further and met a stick, and said to it,
'Stick, stick, beat kid, kid won't go, 'tis a'most midnight, and hame I must go.'
But the stick would not.
She went a little further and met a fire.
'Fire, fire, burn stick, stick won't beat kid, kid won't go, 'tis a'most midnight, and hame I must go.'
But the fire would not.
She went a little further and met with water.

'Water, water, quench fire, fire won't burn stick,' etc.
But the water would not.
She went a little further and met an ox.
'Ox, ox, drink water,' etc.
She went a little further and met a butcher, etc.
She went a little further and met a rope, etc.
She went a little further and met some grease, etc.
'Grease, grease, grease rope.'
She went a little further and met a rat.
'Rat, rat, eat grease,' etc.
She went a little further and met a cat.
'Cat, cat, kill rat,' etc.
The cat began to bite the rat, the rat began to eat the grease, the
grease began to grease the rope, the rope to hang the butcher,
the butcher to kill the ox, the ox to drink the water, the water
to quench the fire, the fire to burn the stick, the stick to beat
the kid, and so the kid went home."

In other accounts of the same tale the kid is a pig, the silver penny a
crooked sixpence; the pig would not go over the stile, and the old woman
could not get her old man's supper ready.

The several prefigurations are not difficult to make out. Very many
of the babblings put into the mouths of English children are of foreign
origin; the story of "The Kid" was known in Leipsic and sung by
German children in 1731, very possibly coming in this way from the
Jewish colony.

In Denmark it is also a favourite with the school children.

The other Jewish rhyme, kept in remembrance by modern Jews, is
printed at the end of their Passover Service in English and in Hebrew.

ONE is known as the Chad Gadyâ. It is an arithmetical poem, and
begins—

"Who knoweth One?"

"I know One, One is God, who is over heaven and earth!"

"Who knoweth two?"

"I know two, two tables of the Covenant, but One is God, who reigneth over heaven and earth!"

When the Latin of our churches was on the lips of everyone in the Middle Ages, an adaptation of this childish creed was taught to little Christians, beginning—

"Unus est Deus,"

but with a Christian theme.

CHAPTER IV.

AN ANCIENT ENGLISH RHYME

From which came the well-known nursery tale of—

"A frog, who would a-wooing go.
Hey, oh! says Rowly.
Whether his mother would let him or no,
With a Rowly Powly Gammon and Spinach,
Hey, oh! says Anthony Rowly."

In 1549 the Scottish shepherds sang a song, entitled "The frog that came to the myl dur." In 1580 a later ballad, called "A most strange wedding of a frog and a mouse," was licensed by the Stationers' Company. There is a second version extant in *Pills to Purge Melancholy*.

The following was commonly sung in the early years of Henry VIII.'s reign:—

"It was a frog in the well, Humbledum, humbledum,
    And the merry mouse in the mill, Tweedle, tweedle, twino.
The frog he would a-wooing ride, Humbledum, humbledum,
    Sword and buckler by his side, Tweedle, tweedle, twino.
When upon his high horse set, Humbledum, humbledum,
    His boots they shone as black as jet, Tweedle, tweedle, twino.

"Then he came to the merry mill-pin,
Saying, 'Lady mouse, be you within?'
Then out came the dusty mouse,
Saying, 'I'm the lady of this house.'

"'Hast thou any mind of me?' asked the gallant Sir Froggy.
'I have e'en great mind of thee,' her ladyship replied.
'Who shall make our marriage?' suggested the frog.
'Our lord, the rat!' exclaimed the mouse.
'What shall we have for supper?' the thoughtful frog exclaimed.
'Barley, beans, and bread and butter!' generously replied Miss
    Mouse.
But when the supper they were at,
The frog, the mouse, and the rat,
In came Gib, our cat,
And caught the mouse by the back;
Then did they separate.
The frog leapt on the floor so flat,
In came Dick, our drake,
And drew the frog into the lake.
The rat ran up the wall,
And so the company parted all."

The rhyming tale of "The frog who would a-wooing go" is similar in every way to the above.

In Japan one of the most notable fairy-tales relates a story of a mouse's wedding.

SONGS OF LONDON BOYS IN TUDOR TIMES.

In the next two reigns, Edward VI. and Philip and Mary's, the musical abilities of the London boy were carefully looked after and cultivated.

The ballads he sang recommended him to employers wanting apprentices. Christ's Blue Coat School and Bridewell Seminary offered unusual facilities for voice training. One happy illustration of the customs of the sixteenth century was the habit of the barber-surgeon's boy, who amused the customers, waiting for "next turn" to be shaved or bled, with his ballad or rhyming verse; and a boy with a good voice proved a rare draw to the "bloods" about town, and those who frequented the taverns and ordinaries within the City.

In the next reign the condition of the poor was much improved; the effect of the land sales in Henry VII.'s reign, when the moneyed classes purchased two-thirds of the estates of the nobility, and spent their amassed wealth in cultivating and improving the neglected lands. This factor—as well as the cessation of the Wars of the Roses—was beginning to work a lasting benefit to the poor, as the street cries of 1557 show, for, according to the register of the Stationers' Company that year, a licence was granted to John Wallye and Mrs. Toye to print a ballad, entitled—

> "Who lyve so mery and make such sporte
> As they that be of the poorest sort?"

"Who liveth so merry in all the land
As doth the poor widow who selleth the sand?
And ever she singeth, as I can guess,
'Will you buy my sand—any sand—mistress?'

Chorus.

"Who would desire a pleasanter thing
Than all the day long to do nothing but sing?
Who liveth so merry and maketh such sport
As those who be of the poorer sort?"

Even Daniel De Foe, writing one hundred and twenty years after, paid a passing tribute to Queen Elizabeth, and said "that the faint-hearted economists of 1689 would show something worthy of themselves if they employed the poor to the same glorious advantage as did Queen Elizabeth."

Going back to the centuries prior to the Tudor period, one is reminded that all the best efforts at minstrelsy—song, glee, or romance—came from the northern counties, or from just on either side the borders.

The prevalence of a northern dialect in the compositions show this suggestion to be in a great degree real. The poems of minstrelsy, however, claim something more than dialect—the martial spirit, ever fever-heat on the borders of the kingdoms of England and Scotland; the age of chivalry furnishing the minstrel with the subject of his poem.

But with the strife of war ended, on Henry VII.'s accession, ballads took the place of war-songs in the heart affections of the people, and they sang songs of peace and contentment. Bard, scald, minstrel, gleeman, with their heroic rhymes and long metrical romances, gave way in the evolution of song and harmony to the ballad-monger with his licence. However, in turn they became an intolerable nuisance, and a wag wrote of them in 1740—

"Of all sorts of wit he's most fond of a ballad,
But asses choose thistles instead of a salad."

Another of the wayside songs of Henry VIII.'s time, sung by man, woman, and child, ran—

"Quoth John to Joan, Wilt thou have me?
I prithee, now wilt? and I'se marry with thee
My cow, my calf, my house, my rents,
And all my land and tenements—
Oh, say, my Joan, will that not do?

I cannot come each day to woo.
I've corn and hay in the barn hard by,
And three fat hogs pent up in a sty;
I have a mare, and she's coal black;
I ride on her tail to save her back.
I have cheese upon the shelf,
And I cannot eat it all myself.
I've three good marks that lie in a rag
In the nook of the chimney instead of a bag."

The London surgeon-barber's boy pleased his master's patrons with a whole host of similar extravagances, but he was not alone in the habit, for so usual was it for the poorest of the poor to indulge in mirth, that literary men of the day wrote against the practice.

In a black-letter book—a copy of which is in the British Museum, date 1560—and entitled, "The longer thou livest more fool thou art," W. Wager, the author, says in the prologue—

"Good parents in good manners do instruct their child,
Correcting him when he beginneth to grow wild."

The subject matter of this book also gives a fair view of the customs and habits of the boys of that age. In the character of Moros, a youth enters the stage, "counterfeiting a vain gesture and foolish countenance, singing the 'foote' or burden of many songs, as fools are wont."

Amongst the many rhymes enumerated by Moros, which he claims were taught to him by his mother, occur: "Broome on the hill," "Robin lend me thy bow," "There was a maid came out of Kent," "Dainty love, dainty love," "Come o'er the bourne, Bessie," and

"Tom a Lin, and his wife and his wife's mother,
    They all went over the bridge together;

The bridge was broken and they fell in,
    'The devil go with all,' quoth Tom a Lin."

Another version, more particularly the Irish one, runs—

"Bryan O'Lynn, and his wife and wife's mother,
All went over the bridge together;
The bridge was loose, they all fell in,
'What a precious concern,' cried Bryan O'Lynn.

"Bryan O'Lynn had no breeches to wear,
So he got a sheep's skin to make him a pair."

This rhyme is evidently much older than the Tudor age, and one is reminded of the time when cloth and woollen goods were not much used by the lower classes. The Tzigane of Hungary to-day wears his sheep-skin breeches, and hands them down to posterity, with a plentiful supply of quick-silver and grease to keep them soft and clean. "Bye baby bunting" and the little "hare skin" is the other nursery rhyme having a reference to skins of animals being used for clothing. But "Baby bunting" has no purpose to point to, unless indeed the habits of the Esquimaux are taken in account. In the list of nursery songs sung by children in Elizabeth's reign, the following extract from "The longer thou livest the more foole thou art" gives four:—

"I have twentie mo songs yet,
    A fond woman to my mother;
As I war wont in her lappe to sit,
    She taught me these and many other.

"I can sing a song of 'Robin Redbreast,'
    And 'My litle pretie Nightingale,'

'There dwelleth a Jolly Fisher here by the west,'
    Also, 'I com to drink som of you Christmas ale.'

"Whan I walke by myselfe alone,
    It doth me good my songs to render;
Such pretie thinges would soone be gon
    If I should not sometime them remembre."

To get back again to the true nursery lyrics, one more marriage game of this period is given, entitled—

"WE'LL HAVE A WEDDING AT OUR HOUSE."

"A cat came fiddling out of a barn
    With a pair of bagpipes under her arm;
She could pipe nothing but fiddle-cum-fee,
    The mouse hath married the bumble-bee.
Pipe, cat; dance, mouse;
    We'll have a wedding at our house."

CHAPTER V.

CAT RHYMES.

The old saying of "A cat may look at the queen" is thus expressed in a dialogue between a ward nurse of Elizabeth's time and a truant tom on its return to the nursery.

"*Ward Nurse*: Pussy-cat, pussy-cat, where have you been?

"*Cat*: I've been to London to see the queen.

"*Ward Nurse*: Pussy-cat, pussy-cat, what did you there?

"*Cat*: I frightened a little mouse from under her chair."

No doubt the incident giving rise to this verse had to do with the terrible fright Queen Bess is supposed to have had on discovering a mouse in the folds of her dress—for it was she of virgin fame to whom pussy-cat paid the visit. It has been asked again and again, "Why are old maids so fond of cats?" and "Why are their lives so linked together?" Maybe it is to scare, as did the cat in the rhyme, "a little mouse from under her chair."

* * * * *

"Ten little mice sat down to spin,
Pussy looked down, and she looked in.

What are you doing, my little men?
We're making some clothes for gentlemen.
Shall I come in to cut your threads?
No, kind sir, you'll bite off our heads."

* * * * *

One more rhyme of Queen Elizabeth's time begins—

"The rose is red, the grass is green,
Serve Queen Bess, our noble queen."

* * * * *

"Kitty, the spinner,
Will sit down to dinner,
And eat the leg of a frog.
All the good people
Will look o'er the steeple
And see a cat play with a dog."

* * * * *

"I love little pussy, her coat is so warm,
And if I don't hurt her she'll do me no harm;
I won't pull her tail, nor drive her away,
But pussy and I together will play."

* * * * *

"Three cats sat by the fireside,
In a basket full of coal-dust;
One cat said to the other,
'Su pu, pell mell—Queen Anne's dead!'

'Is she?' quoth Grimalkin, 'then I'll reign in her stead.'
Then up, up, up, they flew, up the chimney."

∗ ∗ ∗ ∗ ∗

"Great A, little b,
    The cat's in the cupboard
And she can't C."

∗ ∗ ∗ ∗ ∗

"There was a crooked man, and he walked a crooked mile;
He found a crooked sixpence upon a crooked stile.
He bought a crooked cat, she caught a crooked mouse,
And they all lived together in a little crooked house."

∗ ∗ ∗ ∗ ∗

"Ding dong bell, pussy's in the well.
Who put her in? Little Tommy Thin.
Who pulled her out? Little Johnny Stout.
What a naughty boy was that
To drown poor pussy cat!"

Or—

"What a naughty trick was that to drown my granny's pussy cat,
Who never did any harm, but caught the mice in father's barn."

CAT TALE OF DICK WHITTINGTON.

This legend of Dick Whittington is of Eastern origin. The story of the
poor boy whose ill-fortune was so strangely reversed by the performances

of his cat and its kittens finds a parallel in a cat tale found in "Arlott's Italian Novels," published 1485. The Lord Mayor of London bearing the name of Richard Whittington was a knight's son, a citizen of London, and never poor. The possible explanation of the cat in the career of Whittington of London had reference to a coal-boat known as a "cat," and far more likely to make a fortune for the future Lord Mayor than a good mouser would be.

CHAPTER VI.

A CRADLE SONG OF THE FIRST CENTURY.

Many authorities pronounce this lullaby to be of the earliest Christian era. Some believe that in times of yore the Virgin herself sang it to the infant Jesus.

> "Sleep, O son, sleep,
> Thy mother sings to her firstborn;
> Sleep, O boy, sleep,
> Thy father cries out to his little child.
> Thousands of praises we sing to thee,
> A thousand thousand thousands.
>
> "Sleep, my heart and my throne,
> Sleep, thou joy of thy mother;
> Let a soothing, hushed lullaby
> Come murmuring to thy heavenly ears.
> Thousands of praises we sing to thee,
> A thousand thousand thousands.
>
> "May nothing be wanting to thee,
> With roses I will cover thee,
> With violet garlands I will entwine thee.
> Thy bed shall be among the hyacinthus,

84

Thy cradle built up with the petals of white lilies.
Thousands of praises we sing to thee,
   A thousand thousand thousands.

   "If thou wishest for music
      I will instantly call together the shepherds.
      None are before them,
   No mortal sings more holy songs.
Thousands of praises we sing to thee,
   A thousand thousand thousands."

If aught be distinct in this early Christian lullaby, it is that old-time ideas of "stars on high," "the sky is full of sleep," and other similar figures of mythical word-pictures are wanting. A mother's sympathy and affection alone bind together the words of her song in illimitable praises—a thousand thousand thousands.

Milton says—

"But see the Virgin blest
Hath laid her babe to rest."

What a bright sanctified glory the child King brought to his baby throne.

   "Thee in all children, the eternal child. Thee to whom the wise men gave adoration, and the shepherds praise."

What countless hosts of child-bands are ever singing some dreamy lullaby of praise to their child King.

In the pastoral district of Vallauria, in the heart of the Ligurian Alps, within a day's journey from the orange groves of Mentone, a yearly festival takes place, when the children of the mountains sing a stanza recalling the Virgin's song—

"If thou wishest for music I will instantly call together the shepherds. None are before them."

"Lo! the shepherd band draws nigh,
    Horns they play,
Thee, their King, to glorify,
    Rest thee, my soul's delight."

No lyrics of the nursery have come down to us fashioned after the first-century song of the Virgin. The older types have survived, and in such an unvarying mould have they been cast that there is in each European country's song the same old pagan imagery obstinately repeating itself in spite of Christianity, so that the songs of the Christian Church became exclusively the hymns of her faithful people, the carols of her festivals, and in the Middle Ages the libretto of her Church mystery plays, setting forth her history and doctrines to the lower orders. If one were to remove the obstacles of idiom and grammar in the poetry of France, Germany, Italy, Spain, Switzerland, or even Russia, and expose the subject of the theme, a mere skeleton of past delusions would remain.

Long before modern European nations received this imagery of past credulities the poets of Greece and Rome had versified the same old-time beliefs. Before Rome was founded the Etruscan race, who flourished in what is now modern Tuscany, had the Books of the Tages fashioned in rhythmical mould, from which their traditions, ordinances, and religious teachings were drawn. They believed in genii as fervently as a Persian. Here is one Etruscan legend of the nursery, recalling

"How the wondrous boy-Tages sprang out of the soil just previously turned over by the plough in the fields of Tarquinii, and communicated to Lucamones the doctrines of divination, by sacrifice, by flight of birds, and by observation of the lightning, a son of genius and grandson of Jupiter."—*Cic. de Divin.* ii. 23.

It was the ancient tale of "Jack and the Beanstalk."

CHAPTER VII.

JACK RHYMES.

In the preceding chapter it was noted how the wondrous boy-Tages was believed in by the ancients. "Jack and the Beanstalk," our modern tale, though adapted to the present age, is the same legend, and known and told in their own way by the Zulus in South Africa and by the Redskin of North America, as well as to other isolated peoples. In these tales of primitive peoples the same wonderful miracle of the soil's fertility takes place, in the one case by the birth of the boy-Tages, in the other by the marvellous growth of the twisting beanstalks which in one night reach up—up—up to the land of the gods and giants. "Jack the Giant Killer," a similar legend but from a Celtic source, was known in France in the twelfth century, and at that period translated into Latin by Geoffrey of Monmouth. Both "Jack and the Beanstalk" and "Jack the Giant Killer" are found in the folk-lore tales of Scandinavia.

ANOTHER JACK OF THE NURSERY CLASSICS

sprang up into being after the wars of Parliament, when the pleasure-hating Puritan gained an ascendency in the land, and when the pastimes of all classes, but more especially those of the lower orders who had been so happy and contented under the Tudor sovereigns, suffered a miserable suspension. They who were in authority longed to change the robe of revel for the shroud. Not only were theatres and public gardens closed, but a war of bigotry was waged against May-poles, wakes, fairs, church music, fiddles, dancing, puppet shows, Whitsun ales—in short, everything wearing the attire of popular amusement and diversion. The rhyme recording Jack Horner's gloomy conduct was, in fact, a satire on Puritanical aversion to Christmas festivities.

"Jack Horner was a pretty lad, near London he did dwell,
His father's heart he made full glad, his mother loved him well.
A pretty boy of curious wit, all people spoke his praise,
And in a corner he would sit on Christmas Holy-days.
When friends they did together meet to pass away the time,
Why, little Jack, he sure would eat his Christmas pie in rhyme,
And say, 'Jack Horner, in the corner, eats good Christmas pie,
And with his thumb pulls out a plum,
Saying, What a good boy am I.'"

The copy of the history of Jack Horner, containing his witty pranks and the tricks he played upon people from his youth to old age, is preserved in the Bodleian Library.

There are a number of men and women who recall a time when the rhymes of "Jack Horner" and "Jack the Giant Killer" appeared finer than anything in Shakespeare; but this much may be said for "Jack Horner," the cavalier's song of derision at the straight-laced Puritan, that it soon lost its political signification, gradually becoming used as a mark of respect.

"Thus few were like him far and nigh,
     When he to age was come,
As being only fourteen inches high,
     A giant to Tom Thumb."

CHAPTER VIII.

RIDDLE-MAKING.

Riddle-making is not left alone by the purveyors of nursery yarns, though belonging to the mythologic state of thought. The Hindu calls the sun seven-horsed; so the German riddle asks—

"What is the chariot drawn by?"

"Seven white and seven black horses."

The Greek riddle of the two sisters—Day and Night. Another one given by *Diog. Lært.* i. 91, *Athenagoras* x. 451, runs—

"One is father, twelve the children, and born to each other
Maidens thirty, whose twain form is parted asunder,
White to behold on the one side, black to behold on the other,
All immortal in being, all doomed to dwindle and perish."[H]

"The year, months, and days."

* * * * *

An interesting English rhyme says—

"Old mother needle had but one eye,
A very long tail which she let fly,
Every time she went through a gap
She left a bit of her tail in the trap."
                    "Needle and sewing cotton."

                * * * * *

"Purple, yellow, red, and green,
The king cannot reach, nor yet the queen,
Nor can Old Noll, whose power's so great,
Tell me this riddle while I count eight."

                "A rainbow."

This nursery rhyme's date is fixed by the reference to Old Noll, the
Lord Protector.

                * * * * *

"As round as an apple, as deep as a cup,
And all the king's horses can't pull it up."

                "A well."

                * * * * *

"Humpty Dumpty sat on a wall,
Humpty Dumpty had a great fall;
Three score men, and three score more,
Cannot make Humpty Dumpty as before again."

                "An egg."

Or—

"And all the king's horses, and all the king's men,
Couldn't put Humpty together again."

Plutarch says of Homer that he died of chagrin, being unable to solve a riddle.

The Ph[oe]nix myth, once believed in by the Egyptian priests, is now, and had even so long ago as in Herodotus' time, degenerated into a mere child-story of a bird, who lived, and died, and rose again from its own ashes. As a relic of a mysterious faith, this fabulous bird has come down to us with diminished glory each century. Old Herodotus, the father of history, tells us that he saw it once—not the bird itself, but a painting of it—at Heliopolis, the City of the Sun, in Egypt. Even this old Greek historian could not quite believe the current story in his day concerning this bird; that it was supposed to revisit the earth after a five-hundred-year sojourn in the land of gods was to him, at least, a little strange. Pliny, the Roman, likewise gives a description of it. "I have been told," he writes, "it was as big as an eagle, yellow in colour, glittering as gold about the neck, with a body-plumage of deep red-purple. Its tail is sky-blue, with some of the pennæ of a light rose colour. The head is adorned with a crest and pinnacle beautiful to the sight."

Another ancient retells the story somewhat different to both the Greek and Roman historians. Thus runs the Indian version. Bear in mind, however, before reading it, that, like the Second Stone Age people, it was the habit of many races in India to cremate their dead:—

"A high funeral pyre is erected of dry wood, on which the body of the dead is laid, and in course of time after igniting the faggots the corpse is consumed. While this cineration is going on vultures and carrion fowl not infrequently pounce down upon the body, and tear away pieces of flesh from the ghastly, smoking corpse. These charred parts of the body they carry away to their nests to feast upon at leisure. But oftentimes dire results follow; the home of sun-dried sticks and litter ignites, and the bird is seen by some of the superstitious peasantry to rise up out of fire and smoke and disappear."

Then the Ph[oe]nix fable comes to mind, "It is the sun-god; he has thrown fire and consumed the nest, and the old bird," and they hastily conclude that the bird they just now beheld flying away is a new one, and has, in fact, arisen out of the ashes they witnessed falling from the branches of the tall tree. The Ph[oe]nix in truth!

The German child's rhyme, given by Grimm brothers, of

"Ladybird! ladybird! fly away home,"

is not out of place here. It evidences a state of mythologic thought.

"Ladybird! ladybird! pretty one, stay!
Come, sit on my finger, so happy and gay.
Ladybird! ladybird! fly away home,
Thy house is a-fire, thy children will roam.
Then ladybird! ladybird! fly away home.
   Hark! hark! to thy children bewailing."

Yearly, as these harvest bugs, with their crimson or golden-coloured shields, appear in our country lanes, the village youngsters delight in capturing them, and play a game similar to the German child's. They sing—

"Ladybird! ladybird! fly away home,
Your house is on fire, your children will roam,
Excepting the youngest, and her name is Ann,
And she has crept under the dripping-pan."

FOOTNOTES:

H "εἰς ὁ πατήρ, παῖδες δὲ δυώδεκα· τῶν δέ γ' ἑκάστῳ
παῖδες ἔασι τριήκοντ' ἄνδιχα εἶδος ἔχουσαι·
῾Η μὲν λευκαὶ ἔασιν ἰδεῖν· ἡ δ' αὖτε μέλαιναι
᾽Αθάνατοι δέ τ' ἐοῦσαι αποφθίνουσιν ἅπασαι."

CHAPTER IX.

NURSERY CHARMS.

To charm away the hiccup one must repeat these four lines thrice in one breath, and a cure will be certain—

"When a twister twisting twists him a twist,
For twisting a twist three twists he must twist;
But if one of the twists untwists from the twist,
The twist untwisting untwists all the twist."

AN ESSEX CHARM FOR A CHURN, 1650 A.D.

"Come, butter, come; come, butter, come,
   Peter stands at the gate
Waiting for his buttered cake;
   Come, butter, come."

* * * * *

The late Sir Humphry Davy is said to have learnt this cure for cramp when a boy—

"Matthew, Mark, Luke, and John, ease us, I beg!
   The devil has tied a knot in my leg;

Crosses three + + + we make to ease us,
　Two for the robbers and one for Jesus."

A CHARM AGAINST GHOSTS.

"There are four corners at my bed,
　There are four angels there.
Matthew, Mark, Luke, and John,
　God bless the bed that I lay on."

The Matthew, Mark, Luke, and John rhymes were well known in Essex in Elizabeth's time. Ady, in his "Candle after dark," 1655, mentions an old woman he knew, who had lived from Queen Mary's time, and who had been taught by the priests in those days many Popish charms. The old woman, amongst other rhymes, repeated—

"Matthew, Mark, Luke, and John,
　The bed be blest that I lay on."

This was to be repeated yearly, thrice on Twelfth Night, and it would act as a charm until the following year against evil spirits.

In 1601 a charm in general esteem against lightning was a laurel leaf.

"Reach the bays" (or laurel leaves), "and wear one."
　"I'll tie a garland here about his head,
　'Twill keep my boy from lightning."

Even Tiberius Cæsar wore a chaplet of laurel leaves about his neck. Pliny reported that "laurel leaves were never blasted by lightning."

MONEY RHYMES.

"How a lass gave her lover three slips for a tester,
  And married another a week before Easter."

* * * * *

"Little Mary Esther sat upon a tester,
    Eating curds and whey;
There came a big spider, and sat down beside her,
    And frightened little Mary Esther away!"

* * * * *

"Sing a song of sixpence,
    A pocket full of rye;
Four-and-twenty blackbirds,
    Baked in a pie.

"When the pie was opened
    The birds began to sing,
Was not that a dainty dish
    To set before the king?

"The king was in his counting-house,
    Counting out his money,
The queen was in the parlour
    Eating bread and honey.

"The maid was in the garden
    Hanging out the clothes,
Then came a little blackbird
    And snapped off her nose."

In Shakespeare's *Twelfth Night* Sir Toby alludes to the "Sing a Song a Sixpence," Act II., Sc. 3:—

"Come on, there is a sixpence for you; let's have a song."
In Beaumont and Fletcher's *Bonduca* it is also quoted.

* * * * *

"There was an old man in a velvet coat,
He kiss'd a maid and gave her a groat;
The groat was cracked and would not go,
Ah, old man, d'ye serve me so?"

* * * * *

"See-saw a penny a day, Tommy must have a new master.
Why must he have but a penny a day?
Because he can work no faster."

* * * * *

"One a penny, two a penny, hot-cross buns,
If your daughters do not like them give them to your sons;
But if you should have none of these pretty little elves
You cannot do much better if you eat them all yourselves."

Written about 1608:—

"There's never a maiden in the town but she knows that malt's
   come down;
Malt's come down, malt's come down from an old angel to a
   French crown.

The greatest drunkards in the town are very, very glad that malt's come down."

In New York the children have a common saying when making a swop or change of one toy for another, and no bargain is supposed to be concluded between boys and girls unless they interlock fingers—the little finger on the right hand—and repeat the following doggerel:—

"Pinky, pinky bow-bell,
Whoever tells a lie
Will sink down to the bad place,
And never rise up again."

NUMERICAL NURSERY RHYME.

"One, two, buckle my shoe;
Three, four, shut the door;
Five, six, pick up sticks;
Seven, eight, lay them straight;
Nine, ten, a good fat hen;
Eleven, twelve, who will delve?
Thirteen, fourteen, maids a-courting;
Fifteen, sixteen, maids in the kitchen;
Seventeen, eighteen, maids a-waiting;
Nineteen, twenty, my stomach's empty."

BAKER'S MAN.

"Pat a cake, pat a cake, baker's man.
Yes, I will, master, as fast as I can.
Prick it and prick it, and mark it with B,
And toss it in the oven for baby and me."

CHAPTER X.

SCRAPS.

"Oh, slumber, my darling, thy sire is a knight;
Thy mother a lady so lovely and bright.
The hills and the dales and the towers which you see,
They all shall belong, my dear baby, to thee."

* * * * *

"Bye, baby bumpkin, where's Tony Lumpkin?
My lady's on her death-bed, with eating half a pumpkin."

* * * * *

"Nose, nose, jolly red nose.
And who gave thee this jolly red nose?
Cinnamon, ginger, nutmeg, and cloves,
And they gave me this jolly red nose."

* * * * *

Story-telling in the Reformation period was so prevalent that the wonderful tales were satirised in the following rhyme, dated 1588:—

"I saw a man in the moon. Fie, man, fie.
I saw a hare chase a hound. Fie, man, fie.

Twenty miles above the ground. Fie, man, fie.
        Who's the fool now?"

"I saw a goose ring a hog,
And a snail bite a dog!
I saw a mouse catch a cat,
And a cheese eat a rat. Fie, man, fie.
        Who's the fool now?"

* * * * *

A Henry VIII. rhyme:—

"My pretty little one, my pretty honey one,
She is a jolly one, and as gentle as can be;
With a beck she comes anon,
With a wink and she is gone."

* * * * *

"Peg, Peg, with a wooden leg,
    Her father was a miller;
He tossed a dumpling at her head,
    And swore that he would kill her."

* * * * *

"Round about, round about
    Maggotty pie (magpie),
My father loves good ale,
    And so do I."

* * * * *

101

"Old father long-legs will not say his prayers,
Take him by the left leg and throw him downstairs."

* * * * *

"Half a pound of twopenny rice,
    Half a pound of treacle,
Stir it up and make it nice,
    Pop goes the weasel."

* * * * *

In 1754 mothers used to say to their children—

"Come when you're called,
    Do what you're bid,
Shut the door after you,
    Never be chid."

A GAME.

"A great big wide-mouth waddling frog,
Two pudding ends would choke a dog."

* * * * *

"Little Nanny Natty Coat
Has a white petticoat,
The longer she lives
The shorter she grows."

Answer—A candle.

* * * * *

102

"As I was going down Sandy Lane I met a man who had seven wives; each wife had a bag, each bag held a cat, each cat a kit. Now riddle-me-ree, how many were going down Sandy Lane?"

Answer—One going down; the others were going up.

* * * * *

"There was an old woman who lived in a shoe,
She had so many children she didn't know what to do.
She gave them some broth without any bread,
And whipped them all soundly and sent them to bed."

* * * * *

"Robert Rowley rolled a round roll round,
A round roll Robert Rowley rolled round;
Round rolled the round roll Robert Rowley rolled round."

* * * * *

"Little General Monk
  Sat upon a trunk
Eating a crust of bread;
  There fell a hot coal
  And burnt into his clothes a hole,
Now little General Monk is dead.
  Keep always from the fire,
  If it catch your attire
You too, like General Monk, will be dead."

MORE FRAGMENTS.

"With hartshorn in his hand
  Came Doctor Tom-tit,

Saying, 'Really, good sirs,
    It's only a fit.'"

* * * * *

"Cowardly, cowardly custard,
Eats his mother's mustard."

* * * * *

"Tommy Trot, a man of law,
Sold his bed and lay on straw,
Sold the straw and slept on grass
To buy his wife a looking-glass."

* * * * *

"Goosey, goosey, gander,
    Whither shall I wander,
Upstairs, downstairs,
    In my lady's chamber?"

* * * * *

"Dilly, dilly, dilly, dilly,
Come here and be killed."
A nursery-tale rhyme of Henry VIII.'s time:—

"The white dove sat on the castell wall,
    I bend my bow and shoote her I shall;
I put hir in my cloue, both fethers and all;
    I layd my bridle on the shelfe.
If you will any more sing it yourself."

* * * * *

"This little pig went to market,
　　This one stayed at home,
　　This one had a sugar-stick,
　　This one had none,
And this one cried out wee, wee, wee,
I'll tell my mother when I get home."

* * * * *

"Little Bo Peep she lost her sheep,
　　And could not tell where to find them;
Let them alone and they'll come home,
　　Carrying their tails behind them."

* * * * *

"See-saw, Margery Daw, sold her bed and lay in the straw;
Was not she a dirty slut to sell her bed and lie in the dirt?"

* * * * *

"Four-and-twenty tailors went to kill a snail,
The best man among them dare not touch her tail;
She put out her horns like a little Kyloe cow,
Run, tailors, run, or she'll kill you all e'en now."

* * * * *

"I had a little moppet, I put it in my pocket,
　　And fed it on corn and hay,
There came a proud beggar

And swore he would wed her, and stole my little moppet away."

* * * * *

"Hub-a-dub dub,
Three men in a tub,
The butcher, the baker, the candle-stick maker,
They all jumped out of a rotten potato."

* * * * *

"Diddle, diddle, dumpling, my son John
Went to bed with his stockings on;
One shoe off, one shoe on,
Diddle, diddle, dumpling, my son John."

* * * * *

"Jack and Jyll went up the hill
    To fetch a pail of water,
Jack fell down and broke his crown,
    And Jyll came tumbling after."

* * * * *

"Hi diddle diddle, the cat and the fiddle,
    The cow jumped over the moon,
The little dog laughed to see such fine sport,
    And the dish ran away with the spoon."

* * * * *

"Baa! baa! black sheep, have you any wool?
Yes, sir; yes, sir, three bags full,
One for the master, another for the maid,
And one for the little child that cried in the lane."

* * * * *

"Here comes a poor duke out of Spain,
He comes to court your daughter Jane."

* * * * *

"Ride to the market to buy a fat pig,
Home again, home again, jiggerty-jig.
Ride to the market to buy a fat hog,
Home again, home again, jiggerty-jog."

* * * * *

"Cross-patch, draw the latch,
    Sit by the fire and spin;
Take a cup and drink it up,
    And call your neighbours in."

* * * * *

"The man of the *South*[1] he burnt his mouth
    By eating cold plum porridge,
The man in the moon came down too soon
    To ask the way to Norwich."

"Dance a babby diddy,
What'll th' mammy do wi' thee?
Come sit on her lap, theart rosy and fat,
    Dance a babby diddy."

* * * * *

"Dickery, dickery, dock,
The mouse ran up the clock,
    The clock struck one,
    The mouse ran down,
Dickery, dickery, dock.
    The clock struck three,
    The mouse ran away,
Dickery, dickery, dock.
    The clock struck ten,
    The mouse came again,
Dickery, dickery, dock."

* * * * *

"There was an old woman toss'd up in a blanket
    Ninety-nine times as high as the moon,
But where she was going no mortal could tell,
    For under her arm she carried a broom.
'Old woman, old woman, old woman,' said I,
    'Whither, ah! whither, whither so high?'
'Oh, I'm sweeping the cobwebs off the sky,
    And I'll be with you by-and-by!'"
The wildest idea is suggested by the rhyme of—

"We're all in the dumps, for diamonds are trumps,
    And the kittens are gone to St. Paul's;
All the babies are bit, and the moon's in a fit,
    And the houses are built without walls."
The economy of the little boy who lived all alone is seen in—

"When I was a little boy I lived by myself,
All the bread and cheese I got I put upon the shelf."

* * * * *

"Draw a pail of water
For my lady's daughter,
My father's a king and my mother's a queen,
My two little sisters are dressed up in green."

The baby game of tickling the palm of the hand will be remembered
in—

"Round about, round about, runs the little hare,
First it runs that way, then it runs up there."

A PROVERB.

"Needles and pins, needles and pins,
When you get married your trouble begins;
Trouble begins, trouble begins,
When you get married your trouble begins."

A COMPLIMENT.

"The rose is red, the violet's blue,
Pinks are sweet, and so are you."

THE REVERSE.

"The rose is red, the violet's blue,
The grass is green, and so are you."

* * * * *

"Little Tommy Tupper, waiting for his supper,
What must he have?
Some brown bread and butter."

FOOTNOTES:

I *South Devon.*

CHAPTER XI.

SONGS.

"WILL THE LOVE THAT YOU'RE SO RICH IN."

"There was a little man and he woo'd a little maid,
And he said, 'Little maid, will you wed—wed—wed?
I have little more to say than will you—Yea or Nay?
For the least said is soonest mended—ded—ded—ded.'

"The little maid replied, some say a little sighed,
'But what shall we have for to eat—eat—eat?
Will the love that you're so rich in
Make a fire in the kitchen,
Or the little God of Love turn the spit, spit, spit?'"

* * * * *

"Cock-a-doodle doo, my dame has lost her shoe;
My master's lost his fiddling stick and doesn't know what to do.
Cock-a-doodle doo, what is my dame to do?
Till master finds his fiddling stick she'll dance without her shoe.

"Cock-a-doodle doo, my dame has found her shoe, and master's
found his fiddling stick.

Sing doodle, doodle doo—Cock-a-doodle doo,
My dame will dance with you,
While master fiddles his fiddling stick
For dame and doodle doo."

The third-century monarch, King Cole, is seriously libelled in the nursery jingle of—

"Old King Cole was a merry old soul,
    A merry old soul was he,
He called for his glass, he called for his pipe,
    He called for his fiddlers three."

* * * * *

"Rowsty dowt, my fire's all out,
My little Dame Trot is not at home! Oh my!
But I'll saddle my cock and bridle my hen,
And fetch my little dame home again! Home again!
Home she came, tritty-ti-trot,
She asked for some dinner she left in the pot;
Some she ate and some she shod,
And the rest she gave to the truckler's dog.
She took up the ladle and knocked its head,
And now poor dapsy dog is dead!"

* * * * *

"There was a little man and he had a little gun,
    And his bullets they were made of lead,
He went to the brook and shot a little duck
    Right through its head, head, head.

"He took it home to his wife Joan
   And bade her a good fire to make,
While he went to the brook where he shot the little duck
   To see if he could shoot the little drake.

"The drake was a-swimming
   With its curly tail,
The little man made it his mark,
   He let off his gun
   But fired too soon,
And the drake flew away with a quack, quack, quack."

The Creole's slave-song to her infant is built on the same lines, and runs—

"If you were a little bird
   And myself a gun,
   I would shoot you.
Bum! Bum! Bum!

"Oh! my precious little jewel
   Of mahogany,
   I love you
As a hog loves mud."

* * * * *

"Some say the devil's dead,
   And buried in cold harbour;
Some say he's alive again,
   And 'prenticed to a barber."

"I had a little pony, his name was Dapple Grey;
I lent him to a lady, to ride a mile away.
She whipped him and she lashed him,
She rode him through the mire;
I would not lend my pony now
For all that lady's hire."

* * * * *

"Little Blue Betty, she lived in a den,
She sold good ale to gentlemen.
Gentlemen came every day,
And little Blue Betty she skipped away.
She hopped upstairs to make her bed,
But tumbled down and broke her head."

TOM, TOM, THE PIPER'S SON.

"Tom, he was a piper's son,
He learned to play when he was young;
But the only tune that he could play
Was 'Over the hills and far away.'
Over the hills and a great way off,
And the wind will blow my top-knot off.

"Now Tom with his pipe made such a noise
That he pleased both the girls and boys,
And they stopped to hear him play
'Over the hills and far away.'

"Tom on his pipe did play with such skill
That those who heard him could never keep still;
Whenever they heard him they began to dance,
Even pigs on their hind legs would after him prance.

"As Dolly was milking the cows one day
Tom took out his pipe and began to play;
So Doll and the cows danced the Cheshire cheese round,
Till the pail was broke and the milk spilt on the ground.

"He met old Dame Trot with a basket of eggs,
He used his pipe, she used her legs.
She danced, he piped, the eggs were all broke;
Dame Trot began to fret, Tom laughed at his joke.

"He saw a cross fellow beating an ass
Laden with pots, pans, dishes, and glass;
Tom took out his pipe and played a tune,
And the jackass's load was lightened full soon."

"OH DEAR, WHAT CAN THE MATTER BE?"

"Oh dear, what can the matter be?
Oh dear, what can the matter be?
Oh dear, what can the matter be?
    Johnny's so long at the fair.
He promised to buy me a bunch of blue ribbons
    To tie up my bonny brown hair."

SIMPLE SIMON.

"Simple Simon went a-fishing
   For to catch a whale,
All the water he had got
   Was in his mother's pail.

"Simple Simon went to look
   If plums grew on a thistle,
He pricked his fingers very much,
   Which made poor Simon whistle.

"Simple Simon went to town
   To buy a piece of meat,
He tied it to his horse's tail
   To keep it clean and sweet."

"I SAW A SHIP A-SAILING."

"I saw a ship a-sailing,
   A-sailing on the sea,
And it was filled with pretty things
   For baby and for me.
There were raisins in the cabin,
   Sugar kisses in the hold;
The sails were made of silk,
   And the masts were made of gold.
      Gold—gold—gold!
   The masts were made of gold.

"There were four-and-twenty sailors
   A-sitting on the deck,

And these were little white mice,
  With rings around their neck.
The captain was a duck,
  With a jacket on his back,
And when the ship began to sail
  The captain cried 'Quack! quack!'
        Quack!—quack!—quack!
    The captain cried 'Quack! quack!'"

DAVID THE WELSHMAN.

"Taffy was a wicked Welshman,
  Taffy was a wicked thief,
Taffy came to my house
  And stole a piece of beef.
I went to Taffy's house,
  Taffy was in bed,
I got the poker
  And hit him on the head."

Sung in derision along the Welsh borders on St. David's Day. Formerly it was the custom of the London mob on this day to dress up a guy and carry him round the principal thoroughfares. The ragged urchins following sang the rhyme of "Taffy was a wicked Welshman."

"MY FATHER HE DIED."

The historical value of nursery rhymes is incapable of being better illustrated than in the following old English doggerel:—

"My father he died, I cannot tell how,
He left me six horses to drive out my plough,

117

With a wimmy lo! wommy lo!
        Jack Straw, blazey boys.
Wimmy lo! wimmy lo! wob, wob, wob."

Mr. Halliwell dates it as of Richard II.'s time, and this much may be said for this opinion, that there is no greater authority than he on the subject of early English rhymes and carols. Mr. Halliwell also believes that of British nursery rhymes it is the earliest extant. There are those, however, who dissent from this view, holding that many of the child's songs sung to-day were known to our Saxon forefathers. In 1835 Mr. Gowler, who wrote extensively on the archæology of English phrases and nursery rhymes, ingeniously attempted to claim whole songs and tales, giving side by side the Saxon and the English versions. There certainly was a phonetic similarity between them, but the local value of the Saxon, when translated, reads in a strange way, being little more than a protest against the Church's teaching and influence.

"Who killed Cock Robin?" is given at length by Mr. Gowler, as well as many scraps of other nursery rhymes. Mr. Gowler seemed to claim that though the lettered language of each succeeding age fashions afresh, the Baby Kingdom knows no such vocal revolutions.

CHAPTER XII.

SCOTCH RHYMES.

The great and alluring exercise of "Through the needle-e'e, boys" has this immemorial rhyme:—

"As I went up the Brandy Hill
I met my father wi' gude will;
He had jewels, he had rings,
He had many braw things,
He'd a cat-and-nine-tails,
He'd a hammer wantin' nails.
Up Jock, down Tam,
Blaw the bellows, auld man,
Through the needle-e'e, boys!
Brother Jock, if ye were mine,
I would give you claret wine;
Claret wine's gude and fine,
Through the needle-e'e, boys!"

THE SCOTCH VERSION OF BRYAN O'LYNN.

"Tam o' the Lin and a' his bairns
Fell n' i' the fire in other's arms!
Oh, quo' the bunemost, I ha'e a het skin!!
It's hetter below, quo' Tam o' the Lin."

* * * * *

"Cripple Dick upon a stick,
   Sand your soo, ride away
     To Galloway
To buy a pound o' woo."

* * * * *

"Pan, pan, play,
   Pan, pan, play,
And gi'e the bairn meal,
It's gotten nane the day."

* * * * *

"The robin and the wren
Are God's cock and hen."

* * * * *

"Gi'e a thing, tak' a thing,
Auld man's deid ring;
Lie butt, lie ben,
Lie amang the dead men."

The above is said by Scotch children as a reproach to one who takes
back what he gave.

A GRUESOME RIDDLE.

"I sat wi' my love and I drank wi' my love,
   And my love she gave me licht;

I'll gi'e any mon a pint o' wine
    That'll read my riddle right."

A person sitting in a chair made of the bones of a relation, drinking out of the skull, and reading by the light of a candle made from the marrow-bones.

*   *   *   *   *

Street game rhyme, something like the well-known "How many miles to Wimbledon?":—

"King and Queen of Cantelon,
How many miles to Babylon?
It's eight and eight and other eight,
Try to win these wi' 'candle licht.'"

To discover a particular person in the company wearing a ring, Scotch children of last century used to say—

"Two before 1, and 3 before 5,
Now 2, and then 2, and 4 come *belive*.
Now 1, and then 1, and 3 at a cast,
Now 1, and *twise* 2, and Jack up at last."

In the game of Hidee the laddies and lassies cry—

"Keep in, keep in, where'ver ye be,
The greedy gled's seekin' ye."

"WHA'S YOUR DADDIE?"

"Little wee laddie,
    Wha's your daddie?
I cam out o' a buskit, lady,
A buskit, lady's owre fine;
I cam out o' a bottle o' wine,
A bottle o' wine's owre dear;
I cam out o' a bottle o' beer,
A bottle o' beer's owre thick;
I cam out o' a gauger's stick,
A gauger's stick's butt and ben;
I cam out o' a peacock hen."

In Lancashire, where this rhyme is a popular one, the reading differs, "candlestick" being used for "gauger's stick."

"A candlestick is over-fat,
I came out of a gentleman's hat;
A gentleman's hat is over-tall,
I came over the garden wall;
The garden wall is over-high,
An angel dropped me from the sky."

The Scotch "Old Woman who Lived in a Shoe" is a sad jumble of "Old Mother Hubbard" and "Little Blue Betty."

"There was a wee bit wifie
    Who lived in a shoe,
She had so many bairns
    She kenn'd na what to do.

"She gaed to the market
　　To buy a sheep's head,
When she came back
　　They were a' lying dead.

"She went to the wright
　　To get them a coffin,
When she came back
　　They were a' lying laughin'.

"She gaed up the stair
　　To ring the bell,
The bell-rope broke,
　　And down she fell."

"THE MOON IS A LADY."

"The moon is a lady who reigns in the sky
　　As queen of the kingdom of night;
The stars are her army she leads forth on high
　　As bright little soldiers of light.

"Her captains are Jupiter, Saturn, and Mars,
　　Three glittering warriors bold;
And the Milky Way's studded with forces of stars
　　In numbers that cannot be told.

"When Aurora comes up through the Orient gate,
　　And chanticleer crows to the sun,

The moon will retire, and the stars in her wake
  Will follow their queen every one."

R. A. FOSTER^J

FOOTNOTES:

J   When I asked my friend, Robert Adams Foster, whose *Boy Ballads* are being read
   with unusual interest in Scotland, to write a Scotch lullaby, he sent me the above
   verses.

CHAPTER XIII.

A FAVOURITE NURSERY HYMN.

Known to the rustics of England, France, and Italy since the days of the great Charlemagne, has a peculiar history. Like many other rhymes of yore it is fast dying out of memory. The educational influences of the National Schools in the former part of this century, and the Board Schools at a later date, have killed this little suppliant's prayer, as well as most of the other rural rhymes and folk-lore tales handed down by mother to child.

The hymn, though still used in some parts of Northern England, and especially amongst the Nonconformists, as a child's evening ode of praise, runs—

"Gentle Jesus, meek and mild,
Look upon this little child;
Pity my simplicity,
Suffer me to come to Thee."

The next verse, a more modern addition, is—

"Fain I would to Thee be brought,
Lamb of God, forbid it not;
In the kingdom of Thy grace
Give this little child a place."

Leo III. is the supposed author of the book in which it is found, viz., *Enchiridion Leonis Papae.* However, the *Enchiridion* was a book of magic, and not authorised by the Church of Rome, but used by spurious monks and charlatans, wizards and quacks, in their exploits amongst the credulous rural folk. It was full of charms, prayers, and rhymes to ward off evil spirits. The Matthew, Mark, Luke, and John verses are part of the same "Gentle Jesus, meek and mild." The *Enchiridion* was first published in 1532. This hymn was, in the main, derived from the White Paternoster, and handed down to posterity and preserved by the rustics.

THE LATIN VERSION OF THE VIRGIN'S LULLABY.

"Dormi fili, dormi! mater
    Cantat unigenito,
Dormi, puer, dormi! pater
    Nato clamat parvulo:
Millies tibi laudes canimus
    Mille, mille, millies.

"Dormi cor, et meus thronus,
    Dormi matris jubilum;
Aurium c[oe]lestis sonus.
    Et suave sibilum!
Millies tibi laudes canimus
    Mille, mille, millies.

"Ne quid desit, sternam rosis
    Sternam f[oe]num violis,
Pavimentum hyacinthis
    Et praesepe liliis
Millies tibi laudes canimus
    Mille, mille, millies.

"Si vis musicam, pastores
    Convocabo protinus
Illis nulli sunt priores;
    Nemo canit castius
Millies tibi laudes canimus
    Mille, mille, millies."

CHAPTER XIV.

"THERE WAS A MAID CAME OUT OF KENT."

"There was a maid came out of Kent,
    Dangerous be, dangerous be;
There was a maid came out of Kent,
Fayre, propre, small, and gent
As ever upon the ground went,
    For so should it be."
Of authentic currency in Mary's time.

* * * * *

"Martin Smart and his man, fodledum, fodledum;
Martin Smart and his man, fodledum, bell."
Same date.

* * * * *

"I see the moon, and the moon sees me;
God bless the moon, and God bless me."
Child's saying.

* * * * *

"1, 2, 3, 4, 5,
I caught a hare alive;
6, 7, 8, 9, 10,
I let her go again."
Counting-out rhyme.

* * * * *

"Great | A was a | larm'd at | B's bad be | haviour,
Be | cause C | D, E, F de | nied G a | favour;
H had a | husband with | I, J, | K and L;
M married | Mary, and | taught | her scholars | how to spell
A B C, D E F G, H I J K L M,
N O P Q, R S T U, V W X Y Z, Z, Z."

* * * * *

"Hush-a-by, baby, on a green bock (Saxon for bough);
When the wind blows the cradle will rock."

A NURSERY TALE.

"I saddled my sow with a sieve of butter-milk, put my foot into the
stirrup, and leaped up nine miles beyond the moon into the land of
temperance, where there was nothing but hammers and hatchets and
candlesticks, and there lay bleeding Old Noll. I let him lie and sent for
Old Hipper Noll, and asked him if he could grind green steel five times
finer than wheat flour. He said he could not. Gregory's wife was up a
pear tree gathering nine corns of buttered beans to pay St. James's rent.
St. James was in a meadow mowing oat cakes; he heard a noise, hung his
scythe to his heels, stumbled at the battledore, tumbled over the barn
door ridge, and broke his shins against a bag of moonshine that stood

129

behind the stairs-foot door; and if that isn't true, you know as well as I all about it."

* * * * *

"A duck, a drake, a barley cake,
    A penny to pay the baker;
A hop, a scotch, another notch—
    Slitherum, slitherum, take her."

A verse repeated when playing at skimming shells or stones on the water of a pond or lake.

* * * * *

"Hark! hark! the dogs do bark,
The beggars are coming to town.
    There are some in rags,
    There are some in tags,
And one in a velvet gown."

* * * * *

"Bow-wow-wow,
Whose dog art thou?
I'm Tommy Tucker's dog,
Bow-wow-wow!"

Pope wrote an epigram which he had engraved on the collar of a dog, and gave it to H.R.H.:—

"I am his Highness' dog at Kew;
Pray tell me, sir, whose dog are you?"

A B C JINGLES.

"A was an Archer that shot at a frog,
B was a Butcher—he had a big dog,
C was a Captain all covered with lace,
D was a Dunce with a very long face."

"A was an apple pie;
B bit it,
C cut it,
D danced for it,
E eat it,
F fought for it,
G got it,
H hid it," etc. etc.

A CATCH RHYME.

"Tottle 'em, bottle 'em, bother aboo,
Who can count from one to two?"
"I can, I can!" "Do, do."
"One and two—" "See, calf, see,
That's not two, but three, three."
"Three or two's all one to me."

CHAPTER XV.

BELL RHYMES.

The jingle of the bells in nursery poetry is certainly the prettiest of all the features in the poetical fictions of Baby-land.

The oft-repeated rhyme of—

"Ride a cock-horse to *Banbury Cross*,[K]
To see a *fair*[L] lady upon a white horse;
Bells[M] on her fingers and bells on her toes,
She will have music wherever she goes,"

has a charm with every child.

The ride of my Lady of Godiva is fancifully suggested by the Coventry version.

* * * * *

"Bell horses, bell horses, what time of day?
One o'clock, two o'clock, three and away."

* * * * *

"*Gay go up and gay go down*
To ring the bells of London town.

"Bull's-eyes and targets, say the bells of St. Marg'-ret's;
Brick-bats and tiles, chime the bells of St. Giles';
Halfpence and farthings, ring the bells of St. Martin's;
Oranges and lemons, toll the bells of St. Clement's;
Pancakes and fritters, say the bells of St. Peter's;
Two sticks and an apple, say the bells of Whitechapel;
Old Father Baldpate, toll the slow bells of Aldgate;
You owe me ten shillings, say the bells of St. Helen's;
When will you pay me? say the bells of Old Bailey;
When I grow rich, chime the bells of Shoreditch;
Pray when will that be? ask the bells of Stepney;
I'm sure I don't know, tolled the big bell at *Bow*.

"Gay go up and gay go down
To ring the bells of London town."

This almost forgotten nursery song and game of "The Bells of
London Town" has a descriptive burden or ending to each line, giving
an imitation of the sounds of the bell-peals of the principal churches in
each locality of the City and the old London suburbs. The game is played
by girls and boys holding hands and racing round sideways, as they do
in "Ring a Ring a Rosies," after each line has been sung as a solo by the
children in turns. The

"Gay go up and gay go down
To ring the bells of London town"

is chorussed by all the company, and then the rollicking dance begins; the
feet stamping out a noisy but enjoyable accompaniment to the words,
"Gay go up, gay go down."

The intonation of the little vocal bell-ringers alters with each line,

"Pancakes and fritters, say the bells of St. Peter's,"

being sung to a quick tune and in a high key;

"Old Father Baldpate, toll the slow bells of Aldgate,"

suggesting a very slow movement and a deep, low tone.

The round singing of the ancients, of which this game is a fitting illustration, is probably a relic of Celtic festivity. The burden of a song, chorussed by the entire company, followed the stanza sung by the vocalist, and this soloist, having finished, had licence to appoint the next singer, "canere ad myrtum," by handing him the myrtle branch. At all events round singing was anciently so performed by the Druids, the Bardic custom of the men of the wand.

* * * * *

In Lancashire—

"Mary, Mary, quite contrary,
    How does your garden grow?
With cockle shells and silver bells,
    And pretty maids all in a row,"

is one of the songs the cottage mother sings to her child.

The Provençal—

"Ding dong, ding dong,
    Ring the bells of St. John's.
Now they are saying prayers.
    Why ring so high?
    'Tis the little children in the sky!"

* * * * *

"Maids in white aprons, say the bells of St. Catherine's."

* * * * *

Every locality furnishes examples of bell rhymes. Selling the church bells of Hutton, in Lincolnshire, gave rise to this satire of the children—

"The poor Hutton people
Sold their bells to mend the steeple.
   Ah! wicked people,
   To sell their bells
   To build the steeple."

In 1793 Newington Church, London, was pulled down, the bells sold, and the sacred edifice rebuilt without a belfry. The children of the neighbouring parishes soon afterwards jeered at the Newingtonians.

"Pious parson" (they sang), "pious people,
Sold their bells to build a steeple.
A very fine trick of the Newington people
To sell their bells and build no steeple."

In Derbyshire a large number of the churches have bells with peculiar peals—

"Crich has two roller-boulders,
Wingfield ting-tangs,
Alfreton kettles,
And Pentrich pans.

Kirk-Hallan candlesticks,
Corsall cow-bells,
Denby cracked puncheons,
And Horsley merry bells."

The bells of Bow Church ringing out the invitation to Dick Whittington to return to his master's house should not be forgotten—

"Turn again, Whit-ting-ton,
Lord-Mayor-of London."

In New York, U.S.A., the little school urchins sing a bell rhyme of—

"Hark, the merry bells from Trinity
    Charm the ear with their musical din,
Telling all throughout the vicinity
    Holy-day gambols are now to begin."

FOOTNOTES:

K Or Coventry Cross.
L Fine.
M Rings.

CHAPTER XVI.

POLITICAL SIGNIFICATIONS OF
NURSERY RHYMES.

In 1660, when the Restoration of Charles II. took place, the great procession of State to St. Paul's Cathedral called forth this rhyme:—

"Come, Jack, let's drink a pot of ale,
And I shall tell thee such a tale
Will make thine ears to ring.
My coin is spent, my time is lost,
And I this only fruit can boast,
That once I saw my king!"

A Roundhead sneer at the man in the street, after the Royalist rejoicings were over.

In a copy of rhyming proverbs in the British Museum, written about the year 1680, occurs the following Puritan satire on Charles II.'s changeability:—

"A man of words and not of deeds,
   Is like a garden full of weeds;
And when the weeds begin to grow,
   It's like a garden full of snow;
And when the snow begins to fall,

137

It's like a bird upon the wall;
And when the bird away does fly,
   It's like an eagle in the sky;
And when the sky begins to roar,
   It's like a lion at your door;
And when the door begins to crack,
   It's like a stick across your back;
And when your back begins to smart,
   It's like a penknife in your heart;
And when your heart begins to bleed,
   You're dead, you're dead, and dead indeed."

Among Marvel's works (vol. i. pp. 434-5) a witty representation of the king's style of speech is given with the *jeu d'esprit* so distinctively peculiar to Marvel:—

"My proclamation is the true picture of my mind. Some may perhaps be startled and cry, 'How comes this sudden change?' To which I answer, 'I am a changeling, and that's sufficient, I think. But, to convince men further that I mean what I say, these are the arguments. First, I tell you so, and you know I never break my word; secondly, my Lord Treasurer says so, and he never told a lie in his life; thirdly, my Lord Lauderdale will undertake it for me. I should be loath by any act of mine he should forfeit the credit he has with you.'"

In England Charles gave his Royal Indulgence to Dissenters, and granted them full liberty of conscience. They who had been horribly plundered and ill-treated now built meeting-houses, and thronged to them in public. Shaftesbury, who afterwards became a Papist, exclaimed, "Let us bless God and the king that our religion is safe, that parliaments are safe, that our properties and liberties are safe. What more hath a good

Englishman to ask, but that the king may long reign, and that this triple alliance of king, parliament, and the people may never be dissolved?" But Charles had a standing army in Scotland, with the Duke of Lauderdale as Lord High Commissioner, and all classes of people in that country were obliged to depose on oath their knowledge of persons worshipping as Dissenters, on penalty of fine, imprisonment, banishment, transportation, and of being sold as slaves. Persecutions of former times were surpassed, the thumbscrew and the boot were used as mild punishments, the rack dislocated the limbs of those who respected conscience, and the stake consumed their bodies to ashes. Villagers were driven to the mountains, and eighteen thousand Dissenters perished, not counting those who were accused of rebellion. He was "a man of words," and the rhyme of this period depicts his whole character.

* * * * *

Two of the courtezans of Charles II.'s time were Lucy Locket and Kitty Fisher. The following rhyme suggests that Kitty Fisher supplanted Lucy Locket in Charles' fickle esteem—

"Lucy Locket lost her pocket,
Kitty Fisher found it;
Nothing in it, nothing in it,
But the binding round it."

On his death-bed the monarch commended the Duchesses of Cleveland and Portsmouth to his successor, and said to James, "Do not let poor Nelly (Nell Gwynne) starve!" Even their pockets were as badly lined as Lucy Locket's.

The hatred of the Roman Catholic religion "had become," said Macaulay, "one of the ruling passions of the community, and was as strong in the ignorant and profane as in those who were Protestants from conviction." Charles II. was suspected by many of leaning towards the Roman Catholic religion. His brother, and heir presumptive, was discovered to be a bigoted Catholic, and in defiance to the remonstrances of the House of Commons had married another papist—Mary of Modena.

The common people apprehended a return of the times of her whom they unreasonably called Bloody Mary. Sons of this marriage, they feared, meant a long succession of princes and kings hostile to the Protestant faith and government by the people. In 1689, when William of Orange became king in James II.'s place, a political squib went off in the style of a nursery lullaby, entitled "Father Peter's policy discovered; or, the Prince of Wales proved a Popish Perkin"—

"In Rome there is a fearful rout,
And what do you think it's all about?
Because the birth of the Babe's come out!
    Sing, Lalla by babee, by, by, by."

The Douce MS. contains—

    "See-saw, sack a day,
Monmouth is a pretie boy, Richmond is another;
Grafton is my onely joy, and why should I these three destroy
    To please a pious brother?"

At the beginning of this present century the renowned Pastorini contributed his share to simple rhyming. A writer in the *Morning Chronicle* of that period points out Pastorini as being no less a personage than the Right Rev. Charles Walmesley, D.D., a Roman Catholic prelate, whose false prophecies under the name of Pastorini were intended to bring about the events they pretended to foretell—the destruction of the Irish

Protestants in 1825. Just previous to this year every bush and bramble in Ireland had this remarkable couplet affixed to it—

"In the year eighteen hundred and twenty-five
There shall not be a Protestant left alive."

In 1835, when the efforts of the Whig Ministry to despoil the Irish Church proved so strong, a writer in the Press caricatured Lord Grey, Lyttleton, Dan O'Connell, and Lord Brougham in the following nursery rhymes. The attempt was ingenious, but only of small value as showing the rhymes to be the popular ones of that day.

"There was an old woman, as I've heard tell,
She went to the market her eggs to sell."

And—

"Robbin, a bobbin, the big-bellied Ben,
He ate more meat than threescore men;
He eat a cow, he eat a calf,
He eat a butcher and a half;
He eat a church, he eat a steeple,
He eat the priest and all the people."

The other rhymes were—

"There was an old woman went up in a basket
    Ninety-nine times as high as the moon,
Where she was going I couldn't but ask it,
    For in her hand she carried a Brougham!
Old woman, old woman, old woman, said I,
    Why are you going up so high?

To sweep the cobwebs off the sky,
    But I'll be with you by-and-by."

* * * * *

"Old Mother Bunch, shall we visit the moon?
Come, mount on your broom, I'll stride on the spoon;
Then hey to go, we shall be there soon!"

This rhyme was sung at the time in derision to Earl Grey's and Lord Brougham's aerial, vapoury projects of setting the Church's house in order.

"Lord Grey," said the satire-monger, "provided the cupboards and larders for himself and relatives. He was a paradoxical 'old woman' who could never keep quiet."

"There was an old woman, and what do you think,
She lived upon nothing but victuals and drink;
Victuals and drink were the chief of her diet,
And yet this old woman could never keep quiet."

As a prototype of reform this old woman was further caricatured as Madame Reform.

The going "up in a basket ninety-nine times as high as the moon" referred to Lord Grey's command to the English bishops to speedily set their house in order. The ascent was flighty enough, "ninety-nine times as high as the moon, to sweep the cobwebs off the sky"—in other words, to set the Church, our cathedrals and bishops' palaces in order—and augured well; but this old woman journeyed not alone, in her hand she carried a broom (Brougham). It may have been a case of ultra-lunacy this journey of ninety-nine times as high as the moon, and "one cannot help thinking," said a writer of that period, "of the song, 'Long life to the Moon'; but this saying became common, 'If that time goes the coach, pray what time goes the basket?'"

The "Robbin, a bobbin, the big-bellied Ben" parody alluded to Dan O'Connell; the butcher and a half to the Northamptonshire man and his driver; eating "church" and "steeple" meant Church cess.

O'Connell certainly did cut the Church measure about. In his curtailment he would not leave a room or a church for Irish Protestants to pray in.

"Little dog" refers to Lyttleton in the nursery rhyme, for when the under-trafficing came to light, Lord Grey, it is said, was so bewildered at his position that he doubted his own identity, and exclaimed—

"If I be I, as I suppose I be,
Well, I've a 'Little dog,' and he'll know me!"

FINIS

CPSIA information can be obtained
at www.ICGtesting.com
Printed in the USA
BVOW06s1830020817
490965BV00008B/65/P